G.I.I.F.T.S.

God's Infinite Imagination Fulfilled Through Servanthood

By Ebony Vaughan

Scripture quotations marked (NIV) are taken from the Holy Bible, New International Version®, NIV®. Copyright © 1973, 1978, 1984, 2011 by Biblica, Inc.® Used by permission of Zondervan. All rights reserved worldwide. www.zondervan.com The "NIV" and "New International Version" are trademarks registered in the United States Patent and Trademark Office by Biblica, Inc.®

Scripture quotations marked (AMP) are taken from the Amplified Bible, Copyright © 1954, 1958, 1962, 1964, 1965, 1987 by The Lockman Foundation. Used by permission.

Table of Contents

Foreword 1

Acknowledgements 3

Preface 5

CHAPTER 1
The Personification of the Ultimate Gift 7

CHAPTER 2
The Propelling of his Gifts 21

CHAPTER 3
The Power in His Gifts 31

CHAPTER 4
The Purpose of His GIFTS 43

CHAPTER 5
The Price of the Gift 55

CHAPTER 6
The Positioning of His Gifts 65

CHAPTER 7
The Promise That Lies in His Gifts 85

Conclusion 93

Scripture References 95

Sources 106

About the Author 107

Foreword

Never at any time in history has there been a greater need for divine intervention into human affairs than there is now. After perhaps the most challenging year in world history, 2020—the coronavirus pandemic, an economic epidemic, a white supremacy insurrection at the United States Capitol, a record number of deaths, family separations and churches closing down—we need God's divine intervention. In our quest for answers, we must understand that God uses humans to solve human problems. He does it by endowing us with his depository gifts, used for his glory. As Ebony Vaughan so explicitly shares in this book, he uses our "G.I.I.F.T.S." (God's Infinite Imagination Fulfilled through Servanthood). God's plan, purposes and power are revealed through this powerful acronym, G.I.I.F.T.S.

I've known Ebony Vaughan for close to twenty years, and she has dedicated her life to helping people discover, develop, nurture and exercise their God-given gifts in the kingdom of God and the world. Her leadership over our church's Spiritual Gifts Workshop Ministry for many years has afforded her this intimate knowledge, wisdom and understanding of the power of fulfilling your purpose through serving your God-given gifts to the world. Serving faithfully at her local church and heading her own firm as a therapist has given her a rare insight into human behavioral needs. One of those, as shared in her writings, is the need to exercise your gift through compassionate, loving service to others. This is the true Christ model of how we approach our assignment on this planet.

As Ebony masterfully unpacks this pertinent subject, you can sense the inspiration of the Holy Spirit at work. She also gives us a great deal of proof in scripture that when we discover and courageously use the gifts God has given us, lives are saved and everyone profits. Ebony states that "God has so richly positioned his "GIFTS," which are his people, across all the world to bring impact and manifest his glory." This is a great read, not only for believers but for anyone searching for meaning and purpose in this life. As you go through each chapter, you will see that a clear track has been laid for the discovery of your true identity and purpose. A must-read for those seeking to understand God's original intent for his GIFTS to creation and his solution to their present ills.

Dr. Kenneth O. Robinson Jr.

Senior Pastor, Author and Financial Dream Coach

DreamLife Worship Center

Randallstown, MD

Acknowledgements

I give the Lord all the honor for his love and grace shown toward me daily. It is because of the Lord that I am able to labor in this assignment and pour out what I believe is another one of many books that he has deposited into me. God is so faithful!

I thank God for my husband, Vincent, who has been so supportive and truly my think tank in times of questions and doubts! I thank God for his wisdom and advice. I thank God for my children, Joshua and Jessica, my heartbeats. You two are the reasons here on earth that I strive to be my best. I love you with all my heart. I thank God for my mother, and I thank all my family for your love and constant support.

Special thanks to Apostle Kenneth Robinson and Lady Lenyar Robinson for your faithful spiritual leadership in this season of my life. I appreciate your support and prayers.

Finally, I thank God for the many powerful prayers, words of encouragement and support from all my family and friends. Your belief in me has been so inspiring and I will be forever grateful. God has been so good to me and I am eternally thankful for his love shown through his servants.

PREFACE

Everything in this world and on this earth was created by our heavenly father for his good pleasure and divine plan. According to Psalm 24 (KJV), **"the earth is the LORD's, and the fulness thereof; the world, and they that dwell therein."** In understanding this scripture, we see that everything in this world belongs to him. God has a plan and assignment for each of his creations, and it is through this that his intention for servanthood is to be fulfilled. When you gain clarity about what your part is in his plan, it will be one of the greatest discoveries of your life.

I believe that we were created and sent to earth as gifts to carry out the divine plan of God. God has so richly positioned his "GIFTS," which are his people, across all the world to bring impact and manifest his glory. As gifts of God and part of his wonderful creation, we are his intellectual property. We are each a creation of the mind of God, and because of this he has all rights and privileges of the use of us on earth. God has patented us with a divine uniqueness and made us to a standard that can never be copied. We are placed on this earth for a period of time only determined by God to fulfill his plan.

Servanthood is the desire God has for his children and is the key to discovering our purpose on earth. In Matthew 20:28 (AMP), the Bible says**, *"just as the Son of Man did not come to be served, but to serve, and to give His life as a ransom for many [paying the price to set them free from the penalty of sin]"*** —God sent his son Jesus Christ to be for us the perfect example and model of servanthood for all to follow. Servanthood is the basis of a life submitted to God, and it is where we often experience true fulfillment. It is through willfully adopting a lifestyle of servanthood that we as believers serve, worship and fulfill the ultimate call of our heavenly father. So often, people pervert the concept of servanthood and confuse it with inferiority to another or an earthly position. However, in the eyes of God, it is our commission on earth. This book will take us on a journey of just how our heavenly father intends to carry out his assignment on earth through his servants.

CHAPTER 1

The Personification of the Ultimate Gift

God's desire is to see his essence, nature and glory personified on earth through his gifts, his people.

CHAPTER 1: THE PERSONIFICATION OF THE ULTIMATE GIFT

One of the most thought-provoking questions I have had as a believer in my twenty-five years of serving the Lord has been what was in the mind of God when he created his people, who are his gifts. This thought has shaped my study of the spiritual gifts and the fivefold ministry gifts over the last fifteen years. I have become a student of the Bible to gain a better understanding of what the mind of God is regarding his people. Of course, I do not think I have grasped half of the vastness that is in the mind of God. However, I believe that the Word of God gives us a great illustration of God's thoughts for his gifts and his intentions for his creation. What I love about God is that all of his creation is designed not only to meet the needs of other elements of his creation but also to serve as his representative and conduit for growth and development.

I believe that God's creation, which includes his servants, has been commissioned to be his representatives on earth to establish and fulfill his plan. Through this commission, his creation has been given distinct assignments to manifest his glory on earth. When God created man in his image, he endowed him with his infinite wisdom to have dominion and tend to his creation. God endowed man with his essence and nature and provided clear instructions to dominate. The word of God gives us a glimpse of his plan for man. In the book of Genesis, God has established four distinct assignments for his creation. Genesis 1:26–28 (AMP) says, ***"Then God said, 'Let Us (Father, Son, Holy Spirit) make man in Our image, according to Our likeness [not physical, but a spiritual personality and moral likeness]; and let them have complete authority over the fish of the sea, the birds of the air, the cattle, and over the entire earth, and over everything that creeps and crawls on the earth.' So God created man in His own image, in the image and likeness of God He created him; male and female He created them. And God blessed them [granting them certain*** *authority] and said to them, 'Be fruitful, multiply, and fill the earth, and subjugate it [putting it under your power]; and rule over (dominate) the fish of the sea, the birds of the air, and every living thing that moves upon the earth.'"* Through this text, it is clear that there were four assignments given to man: to reflect, rule, reproduce and replenish. These are the ways we personify God on earth. Let's take some time looking at each one in depth.

The assignment to reflect requires us to demonstrate God's likeness and character. We should reflect this not only in how we love others but also in how we carry ourselves in our businesses, families, communities and areas of dominance. It is crucial that the people of God be prepared to demonstrate the likeness and essence of God—1 Corinthians 15:49 says, **"Just as we have borne the image of the earthly [the man of dust], we will also bear the image of the heavenly [the Man of heaven]."** What is the essence and nature of God? Part of the journey of the spirit-filled believer is becoming able to answer this question, based on the Word of God.

When you think of the essence or nature of a thing, you think of what makes it or what it contains. The essence and nature of God can be found in many words—*love, truth, spirit, sovereign, absolute divine*. All of these words and many more define the multifaceted nature and essence of God. God is love. In 1 John 4:7 (AMP), the Bible says, **"Beloved, let us [unselfishly] love and seek the best for one another, for love is from God; and everyone who loves [others] is born of God and knows God [through personal experience]."** If love is from God and when we love we are of God, then this is truly the way we reflect the nature of our heavenly father. So when we look at the first assignment, the first thing he desires for us on earth, it is to love.

The Bible says in 1 John 4:8 (AMP), *"The one who does not love has not become acquainted with God [does not and never did know Him], for God is love. [He is the originator of love, and it is an enduring attribute of His nature.]"* Some of us have a very difficult time with love because we approach it through our soulish or carnal nature, which is impacted by our experiences—any trauma, things we have been through, our values, our morals and what we have been taught by our families and environments. When our soul is impacted by negative experiences, it makes it very difficult for us to love ourselves and others and to experience God's love. Before we are able to, we will have to be transformed by the Word of God and the unconditional love of the father. This transformation requires submitting and yielding to the spirit of God that lives within us. God has given us his spirit, the power source that gives his people the capacity and supernatural ability to reflect his nature and presence on earth, which the spirit-filled believer does through the pursuit of walking in the spirit.

So to experience love is to experience God and to demonstrate love is to be a conduit—the precise channel by which his intention and purpose are demonstrated. Glory to God, we can truly personify his person and his nature. This is absolutely amazing to fathom. As we love and demonstrate his nature, God's power is manifested through his people. Let's look at 1 John 4:12 (AMP), which says, *"No one has seen God at any time. But if we love one another [with unselfish concern], God abides in us, and His love [the love that is His essence abides in us and] is completed and perfected in us."* How awesome, how powerful! Not only do we act as conduits but we also get the incredible privilege of being perfected in love as we demonstrate it daily.

Oxford Languages defines *spirit* as "the nonphysical part of a person which is the seat of emotions and character." The spirit of

God is life giving and empowering, giving a person the ability to see what God sees and to operate on earth with the true authority he has given. The Bible is clear in saying that God is not natural but supernatural; he can only manifest himself on a natural level through his creation. The Bible says in Romans 1:20 (AMP), ***"For ever since the creation of the world His invisible attributes, His eternal power and divine nature, have been clearly seen, being understood through His workmanship [all His creation, the wonderful things that He has made], so that they [who fail to believe and trust in Him] are without excuse and without defense."*** As conduits of his power, we should reflect the true character of our heavenly father, including his spirit and his truth. The Bible is also very clear about the spirit of God living inside each of his creations. We are human, but the spirit of God takes habitation within us, enabling us to function supernaturally as he would. As his creation, we are channels by which his glory is revealed. Because we are the channels by which he is revealed, the people of God have an understanding of the mind of God. As believers we have an advantage over those who are not believers, because we have access to heaven's resources and the mind of God. As we grow deeper in our intimacy and communion with our heavenly father, we gain more knowledge of his thoughts and intentions.

In Isaiah 11:2 (AMP), the Bible says that ***"The life-giving Spirit of God will hover over him, the Spirit that brings wisdom and understanding, the Spirit that gives direction and builds strength, the Spirit that instills knowledge and fear of God."*** This describes what the spirit-filled believer has access to in God. God has given his people his spirit so that they have the capacity to operate as him on earth. Spirit-filled believers possess the intelligence, creativity, ingenuity, innovation and unique thoughts of our creator. He has engineered each of his creations to be a reflection of him in their specific area of rule and assignment on earth, skillfully and deliberately arranged us to operate in the area in which he has called us to. As I studied the word *engineer*, I was struck by many of the associated words: *orchestrated, masterminded, planned, manipulated, maneuvered*. Is this the Word of God in its purest form or what? We are to be a reflection of God in the area which he has engineered us to serve in. God was intentional when he fashioned his creation. He knew his plan and how his promise would be fulfilled through his servants. His idea was always about servanthood. As we go through each chapter of this book, we will gain a clearer understanding of God's infinite imagination and his plan for fulfillment.

Being a reflection has nothing to do with being perfect, but everything to do with a willingness to access and embody the attributes and authority God has given. The intention of God is that the spirit-filled believer reflect his nature by understanding what they now have access to through their covenant. To embrace and embody this concept requires a true act of our will. The more we draw close to him in intimacy and communion, the more we learn about him and gain the capacity to be more like him. When we know him, we are then able to personify the nature and essence of God. We become true representations of God and carriers of his glory, providing proof of God's eternal power. Though we are human, his spirit enables us to experience life supernaturally when we yield to him. What an honor. How amazing is it that God chose us, his creation, to demonstrate himself to those who don't believe? We are a result of God's imagination fulfilled on earth. My God! We personify him through carrying out the four assignments on earth, and it is through these assignments that his intention for servanthood is fulfilled.

The next assignment that God has given the spirit-filled believer according to Genesis 26 is to rule. This means that God has given his people dominion on earth. According to *Merriam Webster, rule* means "to exercise authority or power over [someone or something]." According to Psalm 115:16 (TPT), ***"The heaven of heavens is for God, but he put us in charge of the earth."*** We personify the nature of God by ruling and taking charge on earth.

What I love about our assignment to rule is that it is specific to what God has engineered us for. God would not send you as a gift on earth to rule in an area he has not fashioned you for. Ruling requires us to gain a greater understanding of the gifts and calling of God upon our lives. We rule only within the gifts, talents, expertise and earthly authority that God has given us, the areas in which he has empowered us. It also requires the act of our will to perfect and develop those talents, but this does not negate the supernatural enablement that comes from God. When we operate in the gifts that have been so richly given to us by God, we agree to live a poured-out life. We are containers of God's glory, and when we live a poured-out life, we release all that God has deposited into us for the purposes of serving. Your poured-out and submitted life becomes your worship and service to your heavenly father.

We are God's idea sent to earth to fulfill his purpose. Spiritual gifts are a supernatural grace given to us without personal effort, showing us who God wants us to be on earth. We demonstrate authority and the ability to rule when we operate in our God-given spiritual gifts and talents and bring them to our areas of expertise and professions. In Jeremiah 1:5 (AMP), the Lord told Jeremiah, ***"Before I formed you in the womb I knew you [and approved of you as My chosen instrument], and before you were born I consecrated you [to Myself as My own]; I have appointed you as a prophet to the nations."*** The Lord was speaking to Jeremiah, but I believe that this is what he is saying to all of his children. "When you were in your mother's womb, I knew you and consecrated you, set you aside and called you to..." Can you finish that sentence?

Our spiritual gifts become clearer and more heightened when our faith, connection and relationship with God is increased. It is very difficult to be clear on what your spiritual gift is when you don't know God. The spirit-filled believer should daily develop a connection and a relationship with our creator, which will lead to an increased sensitivity to God through reading his Word, communion and an understanding of our covenant relationship.

God has appointed each one of us to this world for his purpose, and we are to adopt a lifestyle of servanthood in the area he called us to. At first glance, this may appear contrary to God's assignment for us to rule. We rule through the control we are given in the instruction to dominate. When we dominate, it requires us to activate our gifts, talents and expertise to solve problems, to create and to be a resource on earth. The very nature of our dominion is one of servitude to God's plan and its fulfillment.

The spirit-filled believer does not just operate in their spiritual gifts within the four walls of a church; wherever there is a need, God will position his gifts, his people, to bear his nature and function. I can use myself as an example: by profession, I am a social worker, and often my spiritual gifts are manifested in this area. Although I have been formally prepared for this profession, as I yield to the Lord and accept my assignment on earth, I allow the spirit of God to manifest in this area of my life as well. There have been so many times throughout my career when it has been crystal clear to me that the gifts of the spirit were in operation while I was functioning in my position of employment. Others may have assumed that my decisions and actions were just a part of my expertise and knowledge in my field, but I know that not to be the case. Even though I am employed, I see myself as a servant, because everything I do, I do it as unto the Lord. He is the one who appointed me while I was yet in my mother's womb. I believe that this is the posture God desires of his people, for us to see ourselves as servants in whatever capacity we find ourselves in on earth. Colossians 3:23–24 (AMP) says, **"Whatever you do, work at it with all your heart, as working for the Lord, not for human masters, since you know that you will receive an inheritance from the Lord as a reward. It is the Lord Christ you are serving."** This is truly the servanthood that is required of God's people. It is crucial for the spirit-filled believer to understand that God desires all of what we do to be for his glory. Our knowledge and expertise developed on earth through our natural academic efforts and work experiences are not separate from the fulfillment of our assignments on earth. In all we do, servanthood must be the motive.

Your natural talents are also avenues in which you have the ability to rule and serve others. I use the word *rule* because when we are talented in a certain area, we demonstrate mastery. When we demonstrate mastery, we possess extensive knowledge or skill in a subject that can be used for God's glory to address a need and/or solve a problem in the lives of others. There is a difference between spiritual gifts and talents, though it is quite possible for the two to be aligned. I believe that talent is a natural skill that can be perfected over time, but is not necessarily a gift given by God. Spiritual gifts are a grace given supernaturally to the spirit-filled believer to operate in a particular area, not requiring their human effort or knowledge. The more your knowledge of God and your faith increase, the more you'll flow in your spiritual gifts, but your talents increase through practice and developing expertise. You can use both to fulfill God's desire for you to rule.

How can we rule through our spiritual gifts, talents, expertise and professions? In all these areas, there is a level of grace that the spirit-filled believer is able to operate in as they submit themselves to God and see themselves as a servant and conduit fulfilling God's plan. In my experience teaching this biblical principle, I have found that people often struggle with this concept of "ruling" on earth. Oftentimes spirit-filled believers are waiting for permission to rule and to operate in their appointments when God has already given them the ability to do so. Let's look at Psalm 8:6 (NLT): ***"You gave them charge of everything you made, putting all things under their authority"***—we already have permission. Ruling means pouring out in the area which God has assigned us to, knowing that wherever we are, God is, and we are merely a reflection of him.

The third assignment that God has given the spirit-filled believer according to Genesis 26 is to reproduce. This assignment has to do with **creating, multiplying and managing.** The spirit-filled believer uses their gifts and talents to create solutions to life's needs. We are God's intellectual property, his great idea sent on earth. He created us to function as solutions and to paint the canvas of the world that he designed. We are a result of his infinite imagination, and in us dwells infinite knowledge from the visible and invisible world, which we use to create, through procreation, proselytizing and production. Often people stop at procreation—having babies—when they think about the Word of God saying to be fruitful and multiply. However, God also wants us to act as his representatives to carry the good news of the kingdom to convert people into the faith. We reproduce on earth through production as well. We have the spirit of God within us, empowering us with ideas, inventions and innovation, giving us the ability to create.

Another aspect of our assignment to reproduce is to manage, to assume responsibility and authority for a task, assignment or entity. In Genesis 1:28, God said, **"Be fruitful, multiply, and fill the earth, and subjugate it [putting it under your power]."** He gave man the assignment to put all things under their power. When something is under your power, it becomes your responsibility to care for, tend to and see that it flourishes. We assume responsibility in the area which God has given us dominion over and in executing his plan on earth. God only gave man dominion on earth and made him ruler of all of his creation. What an awesome God we serve!

To multiply is to make more of what God has created wherever we abide. He wants us to spread his creativity throughout the earth. Whatever our setting, profession, expertise or passion, we are to see ourselves as creators. And everything we acquire in knowledge, expertise and talents can be used to help someone else. We truly are his servants sent to fulfill his plan on earth.

The fourth assignment is to replenish, meaning to restore and nourish. To *restore* means to bring back to life. You were created to prevent death, decay and destruction to God's creation. The closer we get to God, the more wisdom we gain, and that wisdom is the vehicle to healing. We have the authority and power to bring healing to whatever we are sent to. God has placed his infinite wisdom in his people, giving us the ability to build wherever we are sent. To *nourish* means to sustain by supplying what is necessary for life. God has given each of us the ability to sustain structures and resolve life's problems. He has equipped each of his children with different gifts and talents to enable them to serve in all aspects of society. When we gain this powerful truth about our differences and how we are connected, we become complete, having sufficiency in all things. We become able to embrace the unique gifts and talents of others, and instead of competing or fighting, spirit-filled believers join together. Spirit-filled believers have been given the authority to establish and bring life, order and completion in the areas that God has sent them to.

We have spent a great deal of time on this chapter, looking at how we are to personify God's presence on earth through his four assignments. God's desire is for his creation to personify him so that others are able to experience him. To see ourselves as God's representatives on earth, with the ability to reflect, rule, reproduce and replenish, will require us to maintain faith, elevate our minds and align them with the Word of God. The closer we get to our creator, the more we will be able to see what he sees. Embracing God's infinite imagination fulfilled through servanthood will require us to rise above our soulish limitations and gain a heightened spiritual understanding of the one who created us.

PRAYER:

Father, you so loved the world that you gave your only begotten son that whosoever believeth in you shall not perish but have everlasting life. I thank you for salvation, redemption and sonship. Father, we declare your Word that says we have received the spirit of adoption, whereby we cry Abba, Father. You are our father and creator. I thank you that we have been created after the likeness of you in true righteousness and holiness. I thank you that daily we are being transformed, I thank you that because of your love for your creation we behold your glory daily.

I declare that your people's minds are transformed and that they would not walk after the flesh but the spirit. Give your people a spiritual understanding of who they are and why you created them. Father, help your people to see how they should reflect your image, rule in their earthly assignment, replenish the earth with your glory and goodness and reproduce on earth. Father, give them a fresh and healthy perspective of who they are on earth and the power and dominion that they possess.

Father, I thank you that your people do not have to walk in condemnation, but that you will cause them to be confident in their ability to see themselves as the channel by which your glory is revealed. I declare that the old man is being put off and that the new man will shine forth as they grow closer to you. Father, I declare that your people will walk in wisdom, knowledge, understanding and fear of you as they reflect you on earth.

Father, you said in your Word that you have created man in your own image and in your image you created him. Father, I declare that your people are the light of the world, a city set on the hill. I say that your love is manifested through them daily and that your glory will cover the earth.

In Jesus's name... Amen.

CHAPTER 2
The Propelling of his Gifts

Our ability to carry out our purpose on earth is not just linked to God's plan and desire for us, but to the act of giving ourselves permission to exist as HE has created!

CHAPTER 2 : THE PROPELLING OF HIS GIFTS

In the previous chapter, we talked about God being personified through his people with four major assignments that are found in Genesis. Spirit-filled believers are part of the creation of God, formed in their mothers' wombs and appointed as gifts to this world. Let's review what God told his gift in Jeremiah 1:5 (AMP): *"Before I formed you in the womb I knew you [and approved of you as My chosen instrument], And before you were born I consecrated you [to Myself as My own]; I have appointed you as a prophet to the nations."* God has appointed his children on earth to function as his representatives and carriers of his eternal glory.

Because of this appointment, the spirit-filled believer has been birthed with significance, power, substance and a divine purpose to operate "as" gods on earth, which means that we have been given dominion on earth to rule over the works of what God has created. For the spirit-filled believer, seeing ourselves as gods on earth is a true challenge. Many of us may fear to even communicate this or laugh at the very idea, as it may sound like idolatry or blasphemy. However, it is important for us as spirit-filled believers to truly see ourselves as gifts, with authority and assignment divinely appointed by God. Let's look at Psalm 139:13–17 (AMP): *"For You formed my innermost parts; You knit me [together] in my mother's womb. I will give thanks and praise to You, for I am fearfully and wonderfully made; wonderful are Your works, and my soul knows it very well. My frame was not hidden from You, when I was being formed in secret, and intricately and skillfully formed [as if embroidered with many colors] in the depths of the earth. Your eyes have seen my unformed substance; and in Your book were all written. The days were appointed for me, when as yet there was not one of them [even taking shape]. How precious also are Your thoughts to me, O God! How vast is the sum of them!"*

The spirit-filled believer's ability to carry out their God-given purpose on earth is not just linked to God's plan, but is also contingent on their willingness to give themselves permission to be or exist as God has created them. Existing as God has created requires us to see ourselves from a transformed place. We must see ourselves as having authority and dominion on earth, as the Word of God says, and we have to believe that because of our covenant the same works that Jesus did are in our power also. Do you believe this? Can you see yourself operating in a place of dominion?

Operating "as" gods on earth means we have dominion but not sovereignty. Dominion speaks to rule and authority, while sovereignty speaks to a supreme being with the ability to self-govern. God is, by nature, sovereign. He has absolute power over all creation. Everything was made by him and for him. Colossians 1:16 (AMP) says, **"For by Him all things were created in heaven and on earth, [things] visible and invisible, whether thrones or dominions or rulers or authorities; all things were created and exist through Him [that is, by His activity] and for Him."** Everything that happens, whether bad or good, has permission and access by God. Lamentations 3:37–39 (AMP) says, **"Who is there who speaks and it comes to pass, unless the Lord has authorized and commanded it? Is it not from the mouth of the Most High that both adversity (misfortune) and good (prosperity, happiness) proceed?"** As spirit-filled believers, having dominion has to do with the assignment given to us; we are subject to him and gain access to all through him.

The Holy Spirit resides in us and enables us to function in the capacity that he has sent us on earth to occupy. In Matthew 28:18–20 (AMP), Jesus told his disciples, **"All authority (all power of absolute rule) in heaven and on earth has been given to Me. Go**

CHAPTER 2 : THE PROPELLING OF HIS GIFTS

therefore and make disciples of all the nations [help the people to learn of Me, believe in Me, and obey My words], baptizing them in the name of the Father and of the Son and of the Holy Spirit, teaching them to observe everything that I have commanded you; and lo, I am with you always [remaining with you perpetually—regardless of circumstance, and on every occasion], even to the end of the age." Jesus gave the disciples instructions and empowered them to do as he did, and he assured them that he would always be with them. This is powerful—we understand from it that when God propels us forward, he empowers us with his spirit to accomplish what he wants us to do.

Our functioning as gods on earth is such a delicate topic, when looking from the perspective of the natural mind. To say we are "as" gods would appear to be blasphemy. However, as spirit-filled believers with transformed minds, we understand that this is just the Word of God activated. We must give ourselves permission to function as God has ordained on earth and not be ashamed to operate in our authority wherever God sends us. The basis and foundation of this authority is submission and humility. Spirit-filled believers operate on earth in the name of the Father, Son and Holy Ghost. Our source will always be the supreme God. When we do the works of our Father who sent us, we become as him on earth. Our ability to see ourselves in this capacity has to be developed through our BELIEF and through setting an intention to deepen our relationship with the Father.

In Luke 10:19–20, it says, ***"Listen carefully: I have given you authority [that you now possess] to tread on serpents and scorpions, and [the ability to exercise authority] over all the power of the enemy (Satan); and nothing will [in any way] harm you. Nevertheless do not rejoice at this, that the spirits are subject to you, but rejoice that your names are recorded in heaven."*** In this scripture, Jesus tells his disciples, "demonic spirits are subject to you, but don't get caught up in that—rejoice that your name is written." Jesus wanted his disciples to accept and embrace their kingdom citizenship more than anything. Embracing our identity in Christ will propel us as spirit-filled believers. In the *Merriam-Webster Dictionary*, to *propel* is "to drive forward by or as if by means of a force that imparts motion." As spirit-filled believers, we have been propelled to act as "gods" and representatives made in the image of our sovereign God. This is a form of activation.

In order for the gifts of God to be propelled or mobilized, there must be a belief within them that God has called them and that they are equipped with the power to do what God says. This belief comes from their faith and willingness to trust God. The fact of the matter is we have to give ourselves permission to exist in this authority and be willing to align ourselves with the will of God despite our humanity. The spirit-filled believer will never be able to fulfill their assignment within their own strength, but will need to tap into the supernatural that God has so richly made available to all his gifts. This must be the reality of the spirit-filled believer.

The internal environment of the believer can prevent them from seeing themselves as God has created them. The internal environment is what we think, believe and see. Oftentimes fear, doubt and unbelief exist in our internal environments, making it difficult for us to move forward or operate as God has ordained us. In this state, we often seek to exist in a diminished reality and will prevent ourselves from functioning as God has called us. We get stuck in our humanity, which includes our flaws, insecurities, negative experiences and the identities which we have embraced through our sin nature. We must change the way we see ourselves as we draw closer to our heavenly father. We must possess a spiritual understanding of who we are in God and give ourselves permission to embody that identity. Our internal environment must be faith filled, transformed and aligned with the Word of God. Alignment comes when we live in a place of belief and trust in God. When we are aligned, we see the Word of God in operation in our lives and believe what it says. When the Word of God is in operation, we can be mobilized. Belief and alignment give our heavenly father access; they enable his empowerment and equipping. We will be talking about equipping in later chapters, but the relevant idea here is that God needs our permission for mobilization. Mobilization simply means that the spirit-filled believer becomes God's manifested gift on earth. We allow ourselves to be the conduits of God's power and purpose.

There is a freedom that comes from allowing ourselves to be as God has created us on earth. We are no longer limited by our humanity and the opinions of others. We allow ourselves to be the reflection of our heavenly father, which propels us into his assignment and purpose on earth. As the manifested gifts of God, we exemplify his essence, his greatness and his power **wherever we find ourselves**. My God!

This is so important as we talk about propelling, because so many of us wait for a position or title within the four walls of the church, at our jobs or in our communities to be activated. But God's activation and mobilization don't need to wait on these things—they can come at the point we align ourselves with who he says we are on earth. We serve such a vast God; he is not limited to one space or environment. His gifts are sent to cover the entire earth. So often, we look for recognition and accolades to determine whether we are doing well and are on the right track. I suggest that instead, your intention be to align with God's plan and assignment for your life so that you can experience the fulfillment that can only come from your heavenly father. This is not to say that you won't be recognized or given accolades for the work that you do on earth, but too often we seek validation from people who are not equipped to provide it. Why do I say they are not equipped to provide it? Because more times than not, the people we look to for validation don't have the supernatural knowledge of what's inside us and what we are created for. It's important for us to understand that the approval that is most important in our lives is the approval of the one who created us and sent us on earth to fulfill his plan. God's approval is essential to our fulfillment on earth. Man's approval is great and good to have, but please don't give this priority over the one who created you.

Earlier I talked about the importance of not waiting for a title or position to be mobilized in your particular assignment. Regardless of title, you have the ability to function in the area you abide in at the time you gain knowledge of who you are. Don't ever make assumptions about the areas in which God can use you to bring impact and influence. Yes, there are times when you need a position or title to gain access to a platform or to operate in a particular assignment within a formal structure. This is necessary and expected. You must be willing to go through the process and preparation required to gain access to those formal structures. However, you can also create a platform in the area in which God has you positioned now. Whether in your job, your business or your community, allow the Holy Spirit to manifest through you to bring impact and light. I am so convinced that the world is waiting for the manifestation of the presence of God through his people. Romans 8:19 (AMP) says, ***"For [even the whole] creation [all nature] waits eagerly for the children of God to be revealed."*** God has strategically created his children to manifest his excellence and essence on earth. We are to bring light in dark places and solutions where there are crises.

The propelling of God's gifts comes from the spirit-filled believers understanding who we are in God and being postured for servanthood as God has created us. We serve from our level of assignment, gifting and equipping. Our level of gifting and assignment is determined by our creator, and we become equipped as we submit to his plan and purpose for our lives. We become equipped as we align ourselves with the mind of God and the truth of his Word is activated in our lives.

PRAYER:

Father, I pray that you will continue to enlighten the understanding of your people about your purpose for their lives. Help them to receive the truth of who they are and not be hindered by their humanity and what they once were. Let them receive the adoption of their father and cry "Abba, Father" daily. I pray that as you propel them into their assignment, you cause them to be steadfast and unmovable, always abounding in the works of you.

I declare that they will seek first the kingdom of God and its righteousness and all other things will be added unto them. Help them to worship you, their father and creator, and not the created things.

Father, elevate the minds of your people so that they will be able to know the breadth, depth and mind of you concerning their assignments on earth. I pray that their sensitivity to your voice, presence and direction is increasing daily and that they are not deceived by man's opinion. I come against the spirit of confusion that would hinder them from moving forward and declare that every yoke of bondage in their lives is being destroyed, in Jesus's name.

Father, I declare that your people would be anxious for nothing, but that in everything by prayer and supplication, with thanksgiving, they would let their requests be made known to you so that your peace, which surpasses all understanding, would guard their hearts and minds through Christ Jesus. I declare peace!

Father, I declare that your people would see themselves as servants one to another and that they would not only look to their lives, but that they would do as you have called them to do on earth.

Father, I pray that <u>whatever</u> your people do, let them do it as unto you and not unto man. Let them seek to please you in all they do and not be limited or imprisoned by the opinion of others.

Father, help your people to be sensitive to your timing and not to move ahead of you, for we know that there are many plans in a man's heart, but only yours will stand. We declare it so! Father, we are assured through your Word that your plans for your people are good and that they are plans to prosper and not to harm, plans to give hope and a future.

Thank you, Father, for your love that covers the earth and your people.

In Jesus's name... Amen.

CHAPTER 3
The Power in His Gifts

Live with the understanding that humanity is made up of divine gifts sent to the world with an assignment from God to fulfill his plan on earth!

CHAPTER 3 : THE POWER IN HIS GIFTS

God has equipped all of his children with spiritual gifts and talents that can be used to fulfill his purpose on earth. Spiritual gifts are the manifestation of the Holy Spirit in our lives, the result of a grace given by God to each of us that enables believers to function and operate as his design on earth. Our covenant through the shed blood of Jesus provides us with access, adoption and authority on earth, but it is our clear understanding of who we are in God that gives us clarity about our spiritual gifts. We are his children who have been sent to function on earth as he designed. Many spirit-filled believers spend years serving without that clarity on their function, which results in a feeling of powerlessness and a lack of knowledge of their true purpose in Christ.

Let's look at 1 Corinthians 12:7 (AMP): **"But to each one is given the manifestation of the Spirit [the spiritual illumination and the enabling of the Holy Spirit] for the common good."** It is essential for us as spirit-filled believers to understand that our gifts are to be used to serve others on earth. It is through our servanthood that God's infinite imagination is fulfilled. When we serve, we allow the mind of God to be activated on earth. The spirit-filled believer must give themselves the permission to be the manifested gift on earth, embracing their spiritual gifts and identity as a son or a daughter in God and not walking in fear. The Bible says in 1 Timothy 1:7 (Message), **"God doesn't want us to be shy with his gifts, but bold and loving and sensible."** We are to be deliberate and intentional in our pursuits to function in the position and authority that God has given us. The act of our will and our belief are necessities to accomplishing his plan on earth.

Everything that we are and are equipped to do can be used for God's glory. This is the thing that is so amazing in God's creation and makes us so powerful. We are not all the same, yet all of our gifts come from the same spirit. My God, who can know God! Ephesians 2:10 (NIV) says, ***"For we are God's handiwork, created in Christ Jesus to do good works, which God prepared in advance for us to do."*** We are truly the masterpiece of God, and the purpose of the life of a spirit-filled believer is to function in the power of the Holy Spirit who lives in us. Our true purpose in God is servanthood. The power that resides in us should be poured out through our love and service to others.

I believe it is crucial we understand the power that abides in the spirit-filled believer. We are endowed with power to function as God's design on earth, and it is imperative that we do not attempt to serve in our own strength. Let's look at what the Word says in 2 Corinthians 4:7 (NIV): ***"But we have this treasure in jars of clay to show that this all-surpassing power is from God and not from us."*** Understanding this concept will help the spirit-filled believer not to make the mistake of relying on their own strength and walking in pride. Without the spirit of God, which is our power source, we do not have the capacity to function on earth as he has ordained.

The spirit-filled believer must never stop drawing closer to the heavenly father. Intimacy and communion are key to enabling the power of God to flow through us. The more we commune with him, the more we know him. Think about it—we get to know people by spending time with them. We learn their personalities and proclivities by caring about them and investing in the relationship, through intimacy and seeking a personal connection. I talk a lot about this in my first book, *F.I.G.H.T.,* the more we commune with God, the more we are willing to trust him to move freely through us. Ask yourself, what would your life look like if you allowed the power of God to flow through you daily? How would that look in your job? In your business? In your community?

One of the ways in which the power of God flows in us is through our spiritual gifts. God has placed his power in the spirit-filled believer with the intention of covering the earth with his glory. Let's look at what the Word says in Acts 2:18 (NLT): ***"In those days I will pour out my Spirit even on my servants—men and women alike—and they will prophesy."*** I want you to take a minute and wrap your mind around the idea that God has poured his spirit in you with the sole purpose of it being poured out to those he has assigned you to. This is mind blowing. The power that resides in us is so powerful, and the only way we know what to do with it is by remaining connected to the one who placed it in us. Our ability to remain connected and submitted to the power source will determine our level of "pour." This power magnifies and increases with submission, devotion and obedience.

It is very difficult to talk about the power of God without looking at the concept of spiritual gifts found in 1 Corinthians and Romans. I believe that each spiritual gift described in the Word of God is a characteristic and/or function of the Holy Spirit. These gifts are imparted for his church and his kingdom. It is crucial that I make the distinction of both, because spirit-filled believers must embrace the revelation that God created many of us for his kingdom and not just the church. God sent the spirit-filled believer, who is his gift, imparting them with the function and characteristics necessary to manage, multiply and have dominion on earth. How wonderful is that. Let's look at the Word. Psalm 115:16 (NIV) says, ***"The highest heavens belong to the Lord, but the earth he has given to mankind."*** As the creator, he knew just what he needed for the earth to grow and be sustained. He chose the spirit-filled believers to carry this extraordinary power to spread his glory. My God!

A deep understanding of the spiritual gifts is key to accessing our power in them. There are some amazing books that provide exhaustive studies of the spiritual gifts and how they are manifested in our lives. Lester Sumrall, Don and Kate Fortune, and Archbishop Ralph Dennis are among the many authors whose writings have been useful to me in my studies. Much of the work of these authors I have used to teach about spiritual gifts over the years. Yet I am still grasping the function and operation of God's power in the spirit-filled believer. These powerful spirit-filled authors have produced some wonderful books on this subject and I recommend that you add them to your catalogue.

I also want to clarify something at this juncture. You may notice that I use the word *gifts* in two different senses: to talk about the spiritual gifts and to refer to the spirit-filled believers themselves. This concept comes from the belief that mankind is a direct result of the infinite imagination of our heavenly father. He strategically and skillfully created us (his gifts) for the purpose of filling the earth with his glory. It is important that we are able to see ourselves as the gifts that he has created us to be so that we can also walk with this level of understanding. As a spirit-filled believer, you are a divine creation and gift that God has designed to function and operate on earth. You have divine qualifications for your assignment on earth, which you will find as you discover your spiritual gifts.

The Word of God gives us lots of information about spiritual gifts.

1 Corinthians 12:4–12 (AMP): ***"Now there are [distinctive] varieties of spiritual gifts [special abilities given by the grace and extraordinary power of the Holy Spirit operating in believers],***

but it is the same Spirit [who grants them and empowers believers]. And there are [distinctive] varieties of ministries and service, but it is the same Lord [who is served]. And there are [distinctive] ways of working [to accomplish things], but it is the same God who produces all things in all believers [inspiring, energizing, and empowering them]. But each one is given the manifestation of the Spirit [the spiritual illumination and the enabling of the Holy Spirit] for the common good. To one is given through the [Holy] Spirit [the power to speak] the message of wisdom, and to another [the power to express] the word of knowledge and understanding according to the same Spirit; to another [wonder-working] faith [is given] by the same [Holy] Spirit, and to another the [extraordinary] gifts of healings by the one Spirit; and to another the working of miracles, and to another prophecy [foretelling the future, speaking a new message from God to the people], and to another discernment of spirits [the ability to distinguish sound, godly doctrine from the deceptive doctrine of man made religions and cults], to another various kinds of [unknown] tongues, and to another interpretation of tongues. All these things [the gifts, the achievements, the abilities, the empowering] are brought about by one and the same [Holy] Spirit, distributing to each one individually just as He chooses."

Romans 12:6–8 (AMP): *"Since we have gifts that differ according to the grace given to us, each of us is to use them accordingly: if [someone has the gift of] prophecy, [let him speak a new message from God to His people] in proportion to the faith possessed; if service, in the act of serving; or he who teaches, in the act of teaching; or he who encourages, in the act of encouragement;*

he who gives, with generosity; he who leads, with diligence; he who shows mercy [in caring for others], with cheerfulness."

In these passages, the following gifts have been identified:

The Gift of Word of Wisdom	The Gift of Divers Tongues
The Gift of Word of Knowledge	The Gift of Interpretation of Tongues
The Gift of Faith	The Gift of Help
The Gift of Healing	The Gift of Teaching
The Gift of Working of Miracles	The Gift of Exhortation/ Encouragement
The Gift of Prophecy	The Gift of Compassion/Mercy
The Gift of Discernment	The Gift of Leadership/ Administration

Each of these gifts is given by God as he wills without repentance, meaning that a person's ability to operate and function in any of the above areas does not depend on whether or not they know God or even acknowledge him as their source. There is nothing a person can do to deserve or earn spiritual gifts. God can use all of creation to bless and serve his people without partiality. Some may not agree with this, but how many of you have encountered extremely gifted people who don't profess to be spirit-filled believers but without a doubt have that "it" factor? In some cases, they are able through their gifts, talents and expertise to perform a service or task extraordinarily without any formal education or training. Think about entertainers, artists, creators, inventors, the science that has created some of the world's greatest treatments, procedures and medicine. God's infinite imagination has been imparted unto humanity for the purposes of all his creation.

CHAPTER 3 : THE POWER IN HIS GIFTS

This revelation has allowed me to embrace some marvelous gifts and has enabled me to see them through the eyes of God.

It is so important for us to grasp this concept so that we are not limiting God's hands and his glory. I am always amazed when I hear people say they only want to do business with Christians, their own race, their own culture, etc. Although I can appreciate the devotion and support and see it as admirable to a degree, I wonder if this limits God. Are we putting God's handiwork in a box? What are your thoughts? When you encounter God's gifts, can you see them through the eyes of God or do you label them based upon their stated identity? Can you see the GIFT that God has fashioned? I believe that this "sight" can only be obtained from a spiritual understanding and knowledge of God and his kingdom. I want to remind you of what the Word says in Psalm 24:1 (AMP): *"The earth is the Lord's, and the fullness of it, the world, and those who dwell in it."* All of humanity and creation belongs to God.

Many of us may struggle with this concept, because we have been taught various doctrines that have often sown division rather than unity. I believe that this has caused much confusion among spirit-filled believers and others. I do believe that our knowledge of God as the source, our devotion and obedience, enable us to operate with revelation and illumination that is far above what can be done if we don't acknowledge God. However, we must grasp the concept of the kingdom and understand that God's infinite imagination has resulted in his brilliance, excellence and power being expressed in all of the earth. In Ephesians 3:20 (AMP), the Word of God says, *"Now to Him who is able to [carry out His purpose and] do superabundantly more than all that we dare ask or think [infinitely beyond our greatest prayers, hopes*

or dreams], according to His power that is at work within us." It is that power that is at work in the spirit-filled believer and in all of creation that enables the fulfillment and capacity of God's purpose and plan on earth. The capacity of God's gifts is according to the power that is at work in his people.

Prayer:

Father, I pray that your people will grasp a true understanding of the spiritual gifts and talents that you have imparted unto them. I come against the spirit of fear that would hinder them from receiving your gifts and declare that they stand in power, love and sound mind. I pray that they will have a clear understanding of your purpose for their lives. Father, I pray against self-doubt, unbelief and the low self-esteem that would prevent them from seeing themselves as you see them. I declare that the Holy Spirit dwells in them richly.

Father, I declare that as each of them has received a gift, they would use it to serve others. I pray that your people be good stewards of your grace and that they operate as you have ordained by the strength you so richly supply. Father, I declare that you will be glorified and that the manifestation of your spirit will be for the common good of all people.

Father, I pray that your people will operate in the spirit of love and that they walk in a manner worthy of the calling to which you have called them. I pray that they walk in humility, gentleness, patience, joy, peace and self-control.

Father, I pray that your gifts will commit to equipping others for the work of the ministry and building up the body of Christ in unity. Let them operate in truth according to your Word, that your plans will be fulfilled on earth and that your people will mature spiritually.

Father, I declare that your hand is upon your people and they are as royal diadems in your hands. Thank you, Father, for filling the earth with all things.

In Jesus's Name... Amen.

CHAPTER 4
The Purpose of His GIFTS

God has given us all different abilities and gifts, so that through them we can bring God's love and his presence into the land where we are called.

~Sunday Adelaja

CHAPTER 4 : THE PURPOSE OF HIS GIFTS

God has given all of his creation an anointing and the authority to carry out our assignments on earth. Understanding our spiritual gifts help us to understand our divine function. The Bible says in Romans 12:6 (AMP), ***"Since we have gifts that differ according to the grace given to us, each of us is to use them accordingly."*** In the second half of this scripture it goes on to say that we are to use them in proportion to the faith we possess. From this we learn that we must seek knowledge of what our spiritual gifts are, then we must give ourselves permission to function in them with a sincere intention to serve others. This requires faith in God and belief in ourselves. We must be able to see ourselves as manifested gifts being used to function as God on earth. He imparted himself in us so that we can carry out his plan. How awesome is that!

The purpose of God's gift, which is his people, is to serve mankind. Anything other than that is operating out of the plan of God. As I study the Word of God from Genesis to Revelation, I realize more deeply how spiritual gifts identify the functions of God, our creator. Think about what it took to create the heavens and earth, to populate and establish them. What functions were in operation during the creation? Now, consider that he has imparted us with the Holy Spirit, which gives us supernatural ability to function "as" him on earth. God was the ultimate gift that breathed life into everything, and it is that same life that we now have the capacity to breathe into others for the purposes of carrying out his will on earth.

God uses all that he has created to serve his creation. Whether it is nature for his people's nutrients, the beasts of the field for food, the trees for oxygen, the water for purifying, the sun for vitamin treatment, the seasons of the earth to reset his creation—all things are used for his good pleasure! As a mental health professional, I have taken time to study parts of nature and how they can be used to treat people who may be struggling emotionally and mentally. Being in nature is known to help anxiety and stress. Research has shown that it reduces rumination, which is the persistence of negative thoughts. In some cases, taking walks in nature can lower anxiety and clear the mind. Exposure to the sun provides vitamin D, which helps to recharge people because it is composed of ultraviolet light, which the body needs. The sunrise and sunset remind us that there is a cycle of life that is never ending and each day comes with another chance. Water gives us life and has therapeutic properties of cleansing and healing. Only God could have created all of this for the benefit of his people.

The infinite imagination of our father is simply amazing. Every season, summer, winter, fall and spring, is designed to impact people in different ways, and each is a constant reminder of just how good our God is. The Bible says in Genesis 8:22 (AMP), **"While the earth remains, seedtime and harvest, cold and heat, winter and summer, and day and night shall not cease."** Each season testifies that God has every intention to take care of and maintain his created order, despite the conditions of society and man. The fulfillment of his plan is not determined by his creation but by his sovereignty. It says in Psalm 74:17 (ESV), **"You have fixed all the boundaries of the earth; you have made summer and winter."** Through his creative genius, God created such beauty, such splendor, on earth and then decided to send his gifts in the form of humanity to have authority over it all. Let's look at Psalm 8:6 (NLT): **"You gave them charge of everything you made, putting all things under their authority."** This leads me to my sheer awe of how God has endowed his people with gifts that manifest the supernatural. Not only did he divinely design nature to minister to humanity, but he sent humanity to maintain nature and to serve one another.

CHAPTER 4 : THE PURPOSE OF HIS GIFTS

When we look at the spiritual gifts as functions of the Holy Spirit, it helps us to see God's plan on earth. Let's take some time to explore the function of each spiritual gift. Spiritual gifts are identified within three different categories: motivational, ministerial and manifestational. Motivational gifts are the basis and foundation of all that a person does. These are the gifts that often drive a person's proclivities, interests and profession. They guide the lens through which a person views life and the world. The motivational gifts, which can be found in 1 Corinthians 12 and Romans 12, are as follows:

1. The Gift of Word of Wisdom—the supernatural knowledge of the life of an individual or of a situation with supernatural understanding and divine perspective.
2. The Gift of Word of Knowledge—knowledge of facts that could only have been supernaturally revealed.
3. The Discerning of Spirits—the ability to see through a person and know whether or not he or she is telling the truth.
4. The Gift of Faith—a supernatural ability to trust God for the impossible.
5. The Gift of Healing—a supernatural gift that enables faith to heal sickness and disease.
6. The Gift of Working of Miracles—a supernatural intervention by God in the ordinary course of nature.
7. The Gift of Prophecy—foretelling of the future and the supernatural understanding of the heart and mind of God. Exhorts, edifies and comforts.
8. The Gift of Divers Tongues—a sign gift for the unbeliever. A divine and spiritual communication that is different from the speaker's native tongue.
9. The Gift of Interpretation of Tongues—the supernatural verbalization of the meaning of a message just

delivered to the church in a language the speaker does not understand.
10. The Gift of Helps—a supernatural ability to carry out tasks for the smooth operation of an organization. This divine gift is good for working with the hands in practical ways that help others.
11. The Gift of Teaching—a divine ability to present truths for the discipleship of others.
12. The Gift of Exhortation/Encouragement—a divine ability to encourage others in ways that bring life.
13. The Gift of Compassion/Mercy—a supernatural ability to show love and care to others in ways in which others may not have the capacity to.
14. The Gift of Leadership/Administration—a supernatural ability to lead, direct or instruct.

Each of these gifts has been divinely deposited into God's people as signs for the purposes of establishing and carrying out the will of the Father on earth. Some of these "sign" gifts will be seen more within the walls of a church, but others can be manifested upon any of the seven mountains of society, as described by Johnny Enlow in his book *The Seven Mountain Mantle*. Understanding your assignment and the sphere of influence you have been given is crucial for a spirit-filled believer.

I have taught on this subject for many years and have always been astonished at the gifts of God in operation. I love to study God's creation and feel honored to help others discover their uniqueness. In my professional life, I have been afforded the awesome opportunity to work with some amazing gifts of God. Many of them did not say they had a relationship with God, but did recognize that there was something they were extremely good at and could not explain why. "When did you realize you were good at this?" I would ask them, or "Do you have any formal training?" In these conversations, I would learn that they did not have the knowledge that their talents were from God but they recognized that they were not entirely responsible for their gifts themselves. Are you like that? Do you have gifts or talents and question why or where they came from? Some gifts and talents can be cultivated and developed with dedication and practice, but spiritual gifts are a grace that can only come from our heavenly father, the creator.

Spiritual gifts and talents are to be used for ministry and for service. *Ministry* can be defined as an activity carried out by Christians to express or spread their faith, while *service* is the act of helping or doing work for someone. Ministry is often associated with work done within the four walls of a church, but it doesn't have to be. This is a key point, because spirit-filled believers are often limited by a belief that spiritual gifts are only meant to be manifested inside a church building. This limiting belief has created a great deal of confusion within the body of Christ and has hindered the gifts of God from impacting the world for Christ.

Too often, spirit-filled believers have muzzled or minimized their gifting because they felt that it didn't measure up to what they have seen in their traditional churches or religious communities. Many have grown up within their churches with their eyes set upon the pulpit or other ministry roles and have neglected what God may have been preparing them for outside of the four walls of the church.

Ministerial gifts are what God has established for his church. Although these offices will always be stationed within the church for the purposes of spiritual growth and development of the believers, some of these gifts can be called to the nation and other sects within society as well.

The ministerial gifts are:

- Apostles
- Prophets
- Teachers
- Pastors
- Evangelists

These are often office gifts that God gave, according to Ephesians 4:9–13 (AMP): ***"Now this expression, 'He ascended,' what does it mean except that He also had previously descended [from the heights of heaven] into the lower parts of the earth? He who descended is the very same as He who also has ascended high above all the heavens, that He [His presence] might fill all things [that is, the whole universe]). And [His gifts to the church were varied and] He Himself appointed some as apostles [special messengers, representatives], some as prophets [who speak a new message from God to the people], some as evangelists [who spread the good news of salvation], and some as pastors and teachers [to shepherd and guide and instruct], [and He did this] to fully equip and perfect the saints (God's people) for works of service, to build up the body of Christ [the church]; until we all reach oneness in the faith and in the knowledge of the Son of God, [growing spiritually] to become a mature believer, reaching to the measure of the fullness of Christ [manifesting His spiritual completeness and exercising our spiritual gifts in unity]."***

Now you may recognize some of these gifts from the motivational gift section. The reason for this is that a spirit-filled believer can have a gift in one of these areas and yet not necessarily operate in the ministerial office. For instance, a person under the unction of the Holy Spirit can speak a prophetic word, but that does not mean that they operate fully in the office of a prophet. A person can be a leader and have the ability to shepherd groups and/or organizations yet not operate in the office of the pastor.

I truly believe that there is not a space in the earth that God has not sent his gifts to. I grew up in extremely traditional churches where people were taught that it was not of God to take your gifts outside of the church. For example, if a person could sing, dance or act, they were demonized if they had a desire to share their gifts outside of the church world. Although there are some whom God has called to the church specifically, we must recognize and accept that some are not. This is why it is so important for people to cultivate an intimate relationship with God, so that they gain clarity in their assignment and the sphere to which God has specifically called them.

The purpose of God sending his gifts throughout the earth is to manifest his glory, essence, nature and function. Our creator has a vested interest in his creation. This is why I simply love the book *The Seven Mountain Mantle: Receiving the Joseph Anointing to Reform Nations*, by Johnny Enlow. In this book, Mr. Enlow shares his perspective of God supernaturally placing his people into positions of influence and service in order to save the world and receive the kingdom of God. Mr. Enlow states, "God will raise up his seeing sons and daughters and allow them to shine brighter than the sun with answers and solutions for this world to see how heaven can function on earth. Heaven has all seven mountain realities" (p. 125). The seven mountains of society that he refers to are: (1) Mountain of Government, (2) Mountain of Education, (3) Mountain of Media, (4) Mountain of Economy, (5) Mountain of Family, (6) Mountain of Celebration (arts/entertainment) and (7) Mountain of Religion. In his book, he powerfully illustrates that God manifests the glory of his creativity to reveal his wisdom and understanding, because of his love for all of his creation and so that the world can see all aspects of his nature.

Our divine purpose is to function as God on earth in the sphere that he has sent us to. We all have been given assignments and the ability to function in those assignments as he would on earth. This is the purpose of his people. In my book *F.I.G.H.T.*, I explain that operating on earth without knowledge of who you are is like walking without understanding where you're going or why you are going there. People often struggle to gain knowledge of their purpose because they lack understanding of their function, which can be found in their spiritual gifting and/or knowledge of God. As we talked about in previous chapters, lack of knowledge of or devotion to God does not void you of spiritual gifts; however, it impairs your understanding of the significance of your creation. When God created humanity, he had a specific plan in mind for each of us. Your life is better when you have clarity about God's idea for you on earth. How powerful will we be when we embrace the revelation that our very existence is based upon God's plan to express himself uniquely through us to reach the world. This is truly God's infinite imagination fulfilled through servanthood.

Manifestational gifts are the same as the motivational and ministerial gifts, except that they are not always part of us. They operate through the spirit-filled believer according to the need of the moment and the sovereign will of God. The awesome thing about God is he is able to use whoever and whatever he desires to fulfill his plan on earth and in his people. I may not have the gift of prophecy, but God can use me to speak a word from his heart and mind to bless whom he desires—and in that moment, I would have that manifestational gift. The key to these gifts is a person's availability and willingness to submit to the prompting of the Holy Spirit. Manifestational gifts are God's way of demonstrating his supernatural power and sovereignty through and for his people. Submission to this manifestation is servanthood at its very purest form. How awesome is our God!

Prayer:

Father, I pray for your people that they will have a deepened understanding of your plan and purpose for their lives. Father, I pray that you remove all heresy and errors in doctrine that have shaped the minds of your gifts and caused them to muzzle or minimize the spiritual gifts in them. I overthrow all behaviors that were a result of these beliefs and declare that the spirit of truth abides in each of your children.

Let your children walk in the liberty in which you have set them free, and cause them not to be entangled with the yokes of bondage again. I pray that the truth has set them free and they are free indeed. I pray that you will cause them to flourish and that they will become stable and thrive in their areas of gifting and assignment.

I declare that your people will be planted in the kingdom of God and that they will flourish in all that they do. I declare that as they obey your will for their lives, they will bear fruit and prosper in old age. I pray that they will flourish in their relationships and experience joy and contentment. Father, you have given your people everything they need for life and righteousness, and I thank you for preparing them for your plan.

I declare that your people are allowing the spirit of truth to be their guide and that they will not lean on their understanding. I declare that they will acknowledge you in all their ways that you may direct their paths. Father, I pray that your people would not limit you or prevent the Holy Spirit from moving through them in all environments that they find themselves in. Let a holy boldness come upon your people as they allow you to move through them. Cause them to be bold as lions and harmless as doves. I declare that your people do not operate in fear, because they know that they can do all things through you and that no purpose of yours can be thwarted. Father, thank you that we have this assuredness that your counsel shall stand and your purpose will be fulfilled on earth.

Father, I thank you that you have called your people by your name and created all things for your glory. You have made everything beautiful and appropriate in its time. Father, thank you that you have planted eternity and divine purpose in the heart of your people, which nothing under the sun can satisfy except you. How awesome! Father, only in you can your people discover your divine plan. Father, give us spiritual sight and understanding that we may comprehend your overall plan from the beginning to the end.

Thank you, Father, for your thoughts toward your people. You truly called us while we were in our mother's wombs. Thank you for equipping us with supernatural power that helps us to fulfill your purpose on earth. In Jesus's name... Amen!

CHAPTER 5
The Price of the Gift

God changes caterpillars into butterflies, sand into pearls and coal into diamonds using time and pressure. He's working on you too.

~Rick Warren

CHAPTER 5 : THE PRICE OF THE GIFT

We are divine originals created by God to fulfill his plan on earth. What a hefty and often intimidating charge we have as his children. The idea that we are gifts of God sent to the earth sounds so empowering, yet the price of such an honor can often deter our very acknowledgement of this powerful truth. As I approached this chapter, I grappled with just what direction to take it, because this can be a very painful and vulnerable topic. I would look at the screen but become overwhelmed and move on to another task, then come back later only to feel the same way. I began to reflect upon the pain of my past, the truths I found through scars obtained and inflicted, the lies I told myself and the mess they often created. We love the stories of someone overcoming and the process that led to their victory when we hear it from others, but it is very difficult to go through your own process. It is very challenging to see yourself as a gift after you have been soiled by life's ills. Going through your own process and discovering just how valuable a gift you are from God looks different for each of us. Our process is often associated with price. *Price* is defined as an unwelcomed experience, event or action involved as a condition of achieving a desired end. To say that our experiences are conditions to our ends implies we have to experience the pain or ills of life in order to reach the place of God's fulfillment and promise.

Could it be that my pain, my mistakes, my trauma and the pain I inflicted upon others were all required to get me to a place where I could see myself as a gift from God? Is this so? Could I have discovered the truth of my very existence without the pain in my process?

Many of us who have gone through a great deal of suffering in our lifetimes ask these questions. As I sought the Lord with these thoughts, he reminded me of the precious jewel, the diamond. I began to think about the beauty of diamonds and how they are the most desired among precious stones. This took me to a deep dive of research into the symbolism of the process of refinement in diamonds and how it relates to the spirit-filled believer. It was such a powerful correlation, and I thought, wow, how many of us are able to actually see ourselves as diamonds in the eyes of God? I discovered a great deal of information with a lot of big words and processes that I cannot spell, let alone intelligently articulate. However, I was able to identify key factors that I believe are crucial for us to understand as comparable to that which God sees in his children. First, diamonds are described as being indestructible and invincible. Research says that the only thing that can scratch a diamond is another diamond. When I learned this, I instantly began to understand why the Lord had given me this concept.

Indestructible is defined by *Merriam-Webster* as "incapable of being destroyed, ruined or rendered ineffective." *Invincible* is defined by *Merriam-Webster* as "incapable of being conquered, overcome or subdued." When we look at these two definitions, we understand that diamonds cannot be destroyed. This also speaks to the idea that despite any impacts, blows or cuts to the diamond, it can never be rendered ineffective. The inherent value of a diamond never changes, despite the pressure that it may be subjected to. Like the diamond, who we are as gifts from God can never change, no matter what pressure and process we endure. The authenticity and value of the diamond and the spirit-filled believer are only heightened through the applied pressure, pain and process. Romans 5:3–4 (AMP) states, **"And not only this, but [with joy] let us exult in our sufferings and rejoice in our hardships, knowing that hardship (distress, pressure, trouble) produces patient endurance; and endurance, proven character** *(spiritual maturity); and proven character, hope and confident assurance [of eternal salvation]."*

In my research, I discovered that diamonds only come to the surface through the process of volcanic eruptions. Through the pressure and heat of these eruptions, the diamonds are forced up through the earth. This is also what happens in our lives—the pain and pressure of our experiences often bring us to a place of surrender to God. Think about your life. How many times have pain and the pressures of the world driven you into God's arms? Now ask yourself, could I have grown or developed this way without my negative experiences?

The Bible says in Romans 8:28 (AMP), *"And we know [with great confidence] that God [who is deeply concerned about us] causes all things to work together [as a plan] for good for those who love God, to those who are called according to His plan and purpose."* This scripture helps us to understand that all things can be used for God's purpose and plan. I have often been faced with the question of why God would have allowed me to be born into such a chaotic and abusive family. I have never been able to fully explain, other than to say that God has a way of making the very best out of the worst situations. Despite what we go through and what we experience, it is crucial for us to understand just how indestructible and invincible we have been made to be. There is an indestructible power in us that preserves us through the most painful of times. We have a power that resides in us and a covenant that guarantees our sustainability and victory. 1 Peter 1:23 says, *"for you have been born again [that is, reborn from above—spiritually transformed, renewed, and set apart for His purpose] not of seed which is perishable but [from that which is] imperishable and immortal, that is, through the living and everlasting word of God."* It is through the Word of God and the spirit of God that we are able to persevere. We were truly built to last! When we surrender to God, we often begin the process of refinement and growth. I believe that all of our experiences are a part of the plan of God to bring our true worth, value, strength and power to the surface. Just as that diamond is brought to the surface with heat and pressure.

In my studies, I learned that diamonds undergo extensive excavating, cutting and polishing in the beautifying process. Excavation speaks to clearing away of negative external and internal factors and forces that contaminate the stone so that the diamond can emerge. Isn't this like us? We are God's creation, yet we are born to imperfect and flawed human beings. The environments in which we are born are strategic in God's eyes, as he makes no mistakes. The experiences we face in our families, the values, the beliefs and the relationships prepare us in our process of growth and development. The hardships we face cause our faith to emerge, strengthening us despite the difficulties. Enduring these experiences creates a hope in us that becomes impenetrable as we trust in our heavenly father. In the preparation of a diamond, the cutting process is the peeling away/sawing off of outer layers that may impact the clarity of the stone. In the spirit-filled believer, this speaks to the need to cut away those mindsets, behavior patterns and false belief systems obtained through our negative experiences and sin nature. As we grow and develop, it is important for us to begin to challenge these falsities and replace them with the Word of God. When we shed the things that have proven not to work in our lives, we gain spiritual sight, which enables us to begin to see ourselves the way God originally designed us. I believe that this is synonymous with the polishing process of the diamond. We are talking about refinement. Like the diamond, the more we are cut, polished and excavated, the brighter the shine and brilliance that will emerge from us.

CHAPTER 5 : THE PRICE OF THE GIFT

The final thing I learned about diamonds is something you might remember from the beginning of the chapter: a diamond can only be scratched by another diamond. This is so powerful, because the Word of God states in Proverbs 27:17 (AMP), ***"As iron sharpens iron, so one man sharpens [and influences] another [through discussion]."*** God uses his gifts which are his people to serve, teach and guide one another. God sent his gifts, who manifest his very essence, nature and glory, to equip and mature his people so that they may be able to receive the fullness of him. We are all his children, whether we have the abovementioned functions or not, and God uses us for the purposes of building one another. 1 Peter 4:10 (AMP) says, ***"Just as each one of you has received a special gift [a spiritual talent, an ability graciously given by God], employ it in serving one another as [is appropriate for] good stewards of God's multi-faceted grace [faithfully using the diverse, varied gifts and abilities granted to Christians by God's unmerited favor]."*** God's plan is truly fulfilled when his children grasp his heart and mind regarding servanthood. This is the commission for the kingdom!

Through the analogy of diamonds and God's gifts, we understand just how inherently valuable we are as his creation. The divine creativity of God has fashioned his gifts with power, strength and might. The key is that we must believe this powerful truth and be willing to operate in it daily. To choose to see oneself as an indestructible gift from God empowers a person to live and walk in their inherent value on earth no matter what their circumstances and painful situations. Like the stresses and pressures a stone must endure to become a diamond, what a person overcomes, endures and destroys in their life is often simply the price paid for being the gift God chose to release on earth. Think about it—what price have you paid for being the gift of God?

Prayer:

Father, I thank you for saving your people, for redeeming them, for rescuing them from the destruction of sin and their past. Thank you for preserving your people through the fiery trials of their past. Father, you know everything about each one of your children; you know every hair on their heads. There is nothing about your children that you did not foreknow, and I thank you.

Father, I thank you that you have delivered your people from the guilt, condemnation and shame of their past and that they are now the righteousness of Christ Jesus. Father, your children are holy because you are holy, they are righteous because you are righteous. Because of your love, they now have an identity that is not just natural but supernatural. Father, I declare that because of the adoption that is found in your covenant, they now are new creatures in Christ Jesus. Father, I thank you that because of your power all things are new and old things have passed away. I thank you that your people are now seated in heavenly places and are your rightful heirs. Lord, thank you for this promise.

Father, your Word says that after we have suffered a little while, you, who have called us to your eternal glory in Christ, will restore, confirm, strengthen and establish us. Thank you for the strength and guidance you send us, even in darkness. Your Word says that you came that we might have life and that we would have it more abundantly. I pray that you will fortify your people as they continue to submit and surrender to you. I say that your grace has been sufficient in the lives of your people. Father, thank you for fighting for your people and carrying them through every storm. Your Word says many are the afflictions of the righteous, but Lord, truly you delivered your people from them all. Father, you consistently provide a way of escape for your people, and you make your knowledge and wisdom known unto all those who seek you. Thank you, God.

You said in your Word that those who hunger and thirst shall be filled. Thank you for filling your people. Thank you for restoration. The suffering of your people has produced endurance, their endurance has produced character, and their character daily gives them hope. Father, thank you that your people are as trees that are planted by the rivers of water. Their afflictions and hardships have prepared them for an eternal weight of glory beyond all comparison. Glory to God. Your people shall shine forth as diamonds and they shall be as a royal diadem in your hands. Hallelujah. Thank you, Father.

In Jesus's name... Amen.

CHAPTER 6
The Positioning of His Gifts

Each of us is born with a built-in GPS, God's Positioning System, a sophisticated navigational package that divinely aligns us with people and events and keeps us from losing our way.

~Squire Rushnell

CHAPTER 6 : THE POSITIONING OF HIS GIFTS

God's divine positioning is eternal and based on our blood-brought covenant through the sacrifice of our Lord and Savior Jesus Christ. As spirit-filled believers, we have access to the heavenly realms, and according to the Word of God we are seated in heavenly places. This is essential to understand as we seek to reflect his essence and nature on earth. In order for us to operate in confidence and dominion, we must know our position in God. It is so important that we understand this; otherwise, we may not be operating from a knowledge of where we are rightfully placed. When you don't have a clear knowledge of your position, rights and privileges, you make the mistake of trying to operate either in your own strength or beneath the privilege that you abide in through your covenant with God. Operating in your strength and beneath your privilege can result in a lack of power and direction. As spirit-filled believers, God's positioning should be what we seek, as we understand that it's only in this place that we can truly experience and carry out his purpose on earth.

God's physical positioning of his people also speaks to his desire to carry out his plan and purpose for our lives. God is omniscient, meaning he knows everything. He knows the future of his people and oftentimes stations us in places that prepare us for what is to come. His positioning doesn't always immediately make sense, but when you trust and submit to God's plan, it works to your benefit. In Romans 8:28 (NLT), the Word says, ***"And we know that God causes everything to work together for the good of those who love God and are called according to his purpose for them."*** Spiritual growth is in the mind of God as he strategically positions his people in uncomfortable and strange places. God will never lead us astray but promises to always be with us. We may not always understand why he positions us in certain places, but we can be confident that he will never leave us.

The Bible says in Proverbs 3:5–6 (AMP), *"Trust in and rely confidently on the Lord with all your heart and do not rely on your own insight or understanding. In all your ways know and acknowledge and recognize Him, and He will make your paths straight and smooth [removing obstacles that block your way]."* This is such a reassuring Word, because it encourages us to strengthen our faith so that we trust God's judgment and his divine movement in our lives. Many of us have found ourselves in places and positions in life, maybe as a result of our choices and in other cases by God's divine plan, where we may not have had the best experiences or encountered our desired results. These experiences have left many of us with some pertinent questions for God. Why me? Why did you allow this to happen? Why did you send me here? Why was I born into this family? Have you ever asked God these questions? I believe that many of us have. But God makes no mistakes. God has divinely established each of his people for his purpose and his plan. In this chapter we will take a look at the awesome positioning of God and how he is strategic in establishing and releasing his gifts on earth.

According to Psalm 139, we were skillfully formed and knitted together. He appointed our days and of course had knowledge of his path for us and the roads that we would take. The spirit-filled believer's positioning is solely based on the divine creativity of our heavenly father. God took great thought in creating his people and their individual paths and poured himself, that is the Holy Spirit, into the believer, equipping them for the path set before them. The moment that we leave the womb, we have everything we need to sustain that divine journey. The families we were born into and/or raised by were all part of the plan of our heavenly father. Now, this is very difficult to accept for many who have had bad experiences or experienced a great deal of pain relating to their families of origin. I cannot help but recall the

Word that God gave to the Prophet Jeremiah in Jeremiah 29:11 (AMP): ***"'For I know the plans and thoughts that I have for you,' says the Lord, 'plans for peace and well-being and not for disaster, to give you a future and a hope.'"*** In this Word, there were no contingencies presented, only God's assurance that he had it all planned out and that Jeremiah's destiny was good. We may not always believe this when going through difficult seasons in our lives, but it is important for the spirit-filled believer to grasp. We were not given a promise that God's positioning would always feel good, look good or even make sense, but we have the promise that he will never leave us. The spirit filled-believer has been given the instruction to trust God. The faith walk of the believer must be rooted in trust and hope. Psalm 37:23 (AMP) says that ***"the steps of a [good and righteous] man are directed and established by the Lord, and He delights in his way [and blesses his path]."*** Whatever the path that we find ourselves on, it is crucial that we understand that God has established our way before our entrance into this world.

God desires for his people to follow his instruction and be sensitive to his voice in every place we find ourselves. The Word says that he desires for those who seek him to deny themselves, take up the cross and follow him. This is the instruction the spirit-filled believer is given. However, this is not many people's story. If we are honest, many of us have made decisions in our lives that have taken us down very difficult roads and have appeared to take us farther from our heavenly father. Our pursuits may have caused us to err from good judgment and not follow the precepts of God. Is that you? Do you believe that even in this, God was there? Do you believe that your error in judgement or detour was something God knew you would consider while in your mother's womb? I want you to think about it. In your season of detour, did you see God, did you recognize his presence? Let's go to Psalm 139:8 (KJV), which says, *"If I ascend up into heaven, thou art there: if I make my bed in hell, behold, thou art there."* This psalm of David assures us that wherever we find ourselves, God is there. God never leaves his creation. Our willingness to yield to his instruction is not a prerequisite for his presence and positioning, but a lack of that willingness can diminish our experience of his power and the fruitfulness that true submission often leads to.

God's positioning sets the tone for the plan, purpose and promise he has for each of his creations. From a natural perspective, positioning can be defined by three different aspects: (1) **placement in a position**, (2) **promotion in a particular sector** and (3) **portrayal of a thing**. Although natural, these three aspects of this Word are also applicable in the kingdom of God. Our positioning in God is specific to his assignment and purpose. The interesting thing is that we don't always know why he does what he does.

The first aspect of positioning is **placement**. The conditions, environments and families that God places his people in or allows us to be in are not always what we would choose or even pleasant, yet all are a part of the fulfillment of his plan on earth. In the previous chapter, I talked about the price that is often paid for the assignment and purpose God has for our lives. His movement in our lives and the unique spaces he sends us to may not always be what we desire or expect; however, in his infinite wisdom, God's positioning is necessary to prepare us for the journey that he has set before us.

The path that God has set for each of his children is unique to their divine purpose and should not be hindered by limitations or primitive opinions of religion. God can place or station us as spirit-filled believers in any sector of society with the intent to cover the earth with his glory and infinite wisdom. As we have talked about in previous chapters, people often think the spirit-filled believer is only to be placed within the four walls of the church to serve and fulfill the plan of God. Although I believe that our serving within the church is the intent of God's heart, I also believe that God has stationed his gifts in all seven mountains of society. Yes, that's right—spirit-filled believers have been positioned in the Mountains of Government, Health, Education, Economy, Media, Family, Religion and Celebration (Arts and Entertainment) with the sole purpose of being reflections and channels by which God's infinite wisdom, creativity and power can be manifested. When we understand that God's assignment for our lives can take us down unique paths, into professions and passions that may not be considered traditional or even logical, we free ourselves to truly exemplify him in all that we do. With this freedom, people give themselves permission to be who God has called them to be in whatever environment they find themselves in. There have been so many times in my work when I have sensed the Holy Spirit moving through me providing guidance, direction and knowledge that I did not obtain on my own. To the natural mind, it could have been mistaken for my own expertise or knowledge gained through formal education; however, I knew better. God has strategically placed me in the Mountains of Family and Religion to bring healing and freedom through the power of his Holy Spirit.

You may be in business or employed within the seven mountains and still questioning what God's purpose for you is. Could it be that God has positioned you where you are? Could it be that God called you to that mountain to rule and have dominance? Are you looking through the lens of tradition and expectations of man, or can you see God's purpose being manifested right where you stand? Several years ago, I met a young man in church. He was a faithful servant of God who had a desire to become a preacher.

It was all that he talked about, and he often experienced offense and a sense of rejection because he felt that his spiritual leadership did not see that for him. This caused a great deal of discomfort for him, and he even considered leaving the ministry. He was extremely successful in his profession, with a tremendous amount of innovation and creativity. This man touched the lives of so many and was recognized locally and nationally for developing systems and programs for the community. His gifts, expertise and passion brought so much impact to the institutions he worked for and the people he served. Yet he did not feel that he was in purpose, nor did he see God in what he was doing. He was so focused on what he wanted to do within the four walls of the church and what he thought serving God looked like that he was not able to see the work that God was doing through him in his job in the Mountain of Education. In his words, he did not think that what he did in his profession was spiritual enough or that it was what God wanted him to do. The young man could not see how his work could be an assignment from God and a part of God's purpose for him on earth.

This is the case for many spirit-filled believers. We must get to the place where we understand that God's positioning is strategic. God desires for his infinite imagination to be fulfilled through servanthood in all areas of the earth. Even when we are operating outside of the church, in our businesses or our places of employment, when submitted unto God and doing things as unto him, we fulfill his ultimate assignment of servanthood on earth. This is the spiritual understanding we must have in order to see God's true positioning manifesting in our lives.

God's strategic placement can also be related to the families we are born to and/or raised in. His positioning is not always popular and can often result in pain, challenges and/or obstacles.

Even through the challenges, destiny and purpose can be discovered. Let's look at some popular stories in the Bible that depicted God's divine positioning.

In Genesis 12, God told Abraham to leave his family and what was comfortable. He sent Abraham off with this promise, in Genesis 12:2–3 (NIV): ***"I will make you into a great nation, and I will bless you; I will make your name great, and you will be a blessing. I will bless those who bless you, and whoever curses you I will curse; and all peoples on earth will be blessed through you."*** Now, this promise did not include the minor details of Abraham and his family experiencing a famine or the fact that Abraham was going to be deceptive about who his wife was with Pharaoh. However, God's infinite wisdom sent him with a promise. Why do I bring this up? Often we think that God's positioning will shield us from pain, mistakes and errors in our judgment, but it doesn't. We must understand that all that we experience on our journey, God can use to perfect us. He can also orchestrate the experiences and paths in our lives to help instill character traits that will breed hope, trust, stamina and perseverance in his people. This is an important truth, because so often we get stuck in our sins and mistakes and don't grasp that God is in it all. God's positioning is divine and intentional, yet not always the most desired.

Let's look at Moses in Exodus 2. Moses's mother placed him in a wicker basket on the Nile, where he was found by the maidens of Pharaoh's daughter. His sister, who witnessed it all from a strategic position on the riverbank, was able to get permission for his mother (unknown to Pharaoh's daughter) to nurse him. Moses was raised in royalty, although he was a Hebrew boy. He eventually went on to lead his people out of Egypt and into the Promised Land. Like Abraham's, his journey was not devoid of mistakes, poor decisions and suffering along the way, but God had a plan.

Let's look at the book of Esther. Esther had to live with her cousin Mordecai because of the death of both her parents. She was told to hide her heritage for fear of harm to their people. Despite pain associated with her displacement, God used Esther to get the king to withdraw an order for the general destruction of the Jews throughout the empire.

Let's look at Joseph in Genesis 37, thrown into a pit to die by his own kindred and sold as a slave to the Midianites. Joseph's placement led to him eventually becoming the second most powerful man in Egypt next to Pharaoh, where his presence and position caused Israel to leave Canaan and settle in Egypt.

In all these stories, God's positioning led to these figures being displaced from their families and kindred and experiencing challenges and significant obstacles. They were in God's positioning, yet that did not protect them from discomfort and suffering. In today's terms, Esther and Moses would have been considered orphans. In all these scenarios God had a plan to save his people, express his love and show forth his glory on earth. This is still the plan of our heavenly father for the spirit-filled believer.

Many spirit-filled believers have had the unfortunate experience of being displaced from their biological parents, whether through foster care, adoption or being raised by other family members. This is very painful and brings a great deal of agony and confusion in the lives of so many, leading them to struggle with the spirit of rejection and abandonment. They may have endured maltreatment or deep pain at the hands of those who should have cared for them. These experiences may have led to anger, resentment and even hatred toward God because of the one question: "Why would you allow this to happen to me?" As a clinician, I have had the amazing opportunity of being invited on the journey with so many who are healing from displacement from their biological families. In many cases, the pain that they experienced drove them to high achievement, a deeper commitment to family and an unshakeable sense of faith and purpose. Now this was, of course, after some bumps in the road, mistakes made or even them hurting themselves or others through their decisions. In these stories, some have attested that through it all they know that God ordered their steps. They have testified that their experiences made them strong and nurtured in them a love for life and their ultimate purpose on earth. Some of the most powerful people we see today were orphans or displaced from families at a young age, and through their experiences (whether painful or not), God has used them to be impactful and influential in the lives of others. Some may have even asked God whether, if they had not experienced their pain, they would have taken the path they did. Many have expressed their certainty that their suffering was all a part of God's divine plan.

Sadly, there are also people I have worked with who have had the opposite experience; their pain resulted in a life of underachievement, bitterness or lack of direction. In these cases, their inability or unwillingness to get past their painful experiences has led them to a pattern of self-victimization, low sense of self-worth, destructive behaviors and/or poor decisions. Their lives have been filled with sadness, disappointment, resentment and lack of trust, and this lack of trust has prevented them from receiving the love from others that God may have placed along their path to help them. They may not trust God himself. I believe that God is still with them, but they must reach a place of willingness and surrender to experience the life that God has designed for them. It will not be until they give themselves permission to get over their pain that they will be able to receive God's love and healing power and see their experiences as a part of the plan of God for them. This is definitely a process.

Often we find ourselves in difficult places, but they are a part of our process of becoming. God doesn't desire for his people to be abused, tortured and or abandoned; however, because of humanity and the free will given to all, these things happen. God in his infinite wisdom enables something good and beautiful to be birthed through our pain if we let him. God can use all things for his plan to prosper, build and establish his divine will through us.

I want to pause here to pray for those who may be reading who have suffered from abandonment, rejection or displacement as a child.

Father, in the name of Jesus, I pray for your people who may be experiencing anger, disappointment and pain as a result of being displaced from their families. I pray that you will deliver them from the spirit of abandonment, rejection and anger, in the name of Jesus. I pray that you will heal them from the pain caused by their biological families and others and that you will renew the spirit of their minds in Christ Jesus. I pray that you will release your power, strength and might in their lives and cause them to rise above what has been done to them. I decree this day that they are no longer victims but are victors in Christ Jesus. I declare that you will cleanse them of all resentment, bitterness and unforgiveness that has caused them to remain stuck in their past and decree that today is a NEW day. I declare that love has entered their hearts today and that you will envelop them fully with your compassion and mercy. Father, I pray that your strength will be made perfect in their weakness, in Jesus's name. Let them find joy and comfort in the place that you have them in right now, in Jesus's name. Glory to God!

Divine positioning can be exciting but also a very difficult topic, because God's plan and what he allows to happen in the lives of his people cannot always be explained or justified by the natural man. We often associate God with his goodness and blessings, but not with challenges and obstacles. To say that God placed us somewhere often suggests that things will run smoothly and be perfect. It may give us the idea that we will not experience any hardship. But this is just not the case. Our journey through purpose will take us through various paths, roads and conditions; however, if we can see God in it all, it will help us maintain a spiritual lens and an unwavering faith that will cause us to trust God in everything. Psalm 34:19 (AMP) says, *"Many hardships and perplexing circumstances confront the righteous, but the Lord rescues him from them all."*

The next aspect of God's positioning to address is **promotion**. Psalm 75:6–7 (KJV) says, *"For promotion cometh neither from the east, nor from the west, nor from the south. But God is the judge: he putteth down one, and setteth up another."* In this passage, God is letting us know that he is the ultimate authority, with the ability to raise up and to humble. He is the author and finisher of our faith, and there is an appointed time for us all. *Promotion* can be defined in two ways, according to *Oxford Languages Dictionary*: "the action of raising someone to a higher position or rank" and "the action of publicization of a product (can be a person), organization or venture so as to increase public awareness."

During our journey in God, many of us have the desire to be known or famous. We often wish to be promoted in position or rank—sometimes without going through the proper process that God uses to perfect us. In my book *F.I.G.H.T.*, I talked about the power that is gained through preparation and the importance of allowing God to use your experiences in life to develop character. I also stated that often we do not flourish because we move ahead of God or attempt to circumvent his process (*F.I.G.H.T.*, pg. 67). We must not attempt to cheat the process of promotion that comes from diligence. The Bible says in Proverbs 21:5 (AMP), ***"The plans of the diligent lead surely to abundance and advantage, but everyone who acts in haste comes surely to poverty."*** God requires our diligence and that we act not with a motive to be promoted but as unto him. Colossians 3:23 says, ***"Whatever you do [whatever your task may be], work from the soul [that is, put in your very best effort], as [something done] for the Lord and not for men."*** As spirit-filled believers, everything we do must be done as unto the Lord, and in this our motive aligns with his. Diligence is truly a powerful aspect of God's positioning as it relates to promotion.

Spiritual promotion can look very different from natural promotion. We often seek higher positions in rank without understanding the cost of that advancement. From the natural perspective, you might see a promotion as a step up the corporate ladder or a better role within an organization, but the responsibilities of that role may require more time and capacity, taking you away from God's desired plan for you. This is why it is important for us to be sensitive to the movement of God in our lives.

I once was offered such a position. This position was very appealing and came with more money, status and authority within the organization. I wanted so badly to take it, but I just did not feel peace to do so. I had been on the job for several years and had worked really hard, and quite frankly I thought I deserved the promotion. I was approached by an executive and asked if I would consider it. I prayed about it and decided to go to the interview. Keep in mind, I thought I deserved it, which meant I wanted it. However, when I sought the Lord regarding this promotion, I did not sense a release to take it. I went back and pondered for days, and each time, I just did not hear a yes. Finally, I heard the answer I did not want to hear from God. " No, wait." Now I can honestly say that although I wanted the job, there was a peace that came over me when I declined that I cannot explain. Somehow I knew it was going to be OK and that God had something better in store for me. In due time, God showed me what that was. He opened up the door for a position that had far less responsibility, yet freed up my time, which enabled me to start a business.

This experience taught me that God's way is best but we must trust him. That position I felt I deserved was higher in rank, but I was still an employee. He freed up my time to make me an owner with employees of my own. Is that promotion or what! This was an example in my life of God's positioning. When looking for God's positioning in your life, never underestimate the power of prayer and obedience. There is truly a reward in your obedience to God. The key is in cultivating an intimate relationship with him so that you are able to detect his voice and timing in your life. I talk in great detail about this in my first book, *F.I.G.H.T.* When we do things in God's way and in his timing, he has a way of accelerating us beyond human comprehension. It is essential that we have this proper perspective of God's positioning.

The last aspect of God's positioning is his divine **portrayal** of his people. *Portrayal* is defined in *Oxford Languages* as "a depiction of something in a work of art." God desires for the world to see him reflected through his manifested gifts. His intention is to see the spirit-filled believer manifesting his glory, essence and nature. God wants to cover the earth with his love and goodness. He does not position his people in power, influence and authority so that they can become famous or make names for themselves, although this comes with the territory. God's desire is to show forth his divine creativity, ingenuity and innovation throughout all the earth through his people.

In this divine demonstration of his sovereign power, God's desire is for his people to possess good character and a servant's heart with the intention of carrying out his purpose and plan. The Bible says in Proverbs 2:20–21 (AMP), ***"So you will walk in the way of good men [that is, those of personal integrity, moral courage and honorable character], And keep to the paths of the righteous. For the upright [those who are in right standing with God] will live in the land and those [of integrity] who are blameless [in God's sight] will remain in it."*** God desires for his people to demonstrate his character on earth. Too often we see extremely gifted people whose character cannot sustain their God-given gift, and as a result they are found in scandal and in the exploitation of others. This is sometimes why God's gifts are not put on display by God or positioned in places of prominence. There are times when God will keep a person in a lower position or outside of public awareness because of a lack of integrity or love. Too often we see this in the world, where man appoints people in places of prominence and stature. There are times when God will still use these people to bless his people, but if they refuse to change, we often witness their public demise as a result of scandal or some form of impropriety.

God does not intend for his gifts to be without integrity, to exalt themselves or to be made idols by others. God will not compete with his people for his glory. There are times when God will not promote a person because their heart is not in alignment with his. When a person's heart is not pure, they often become prideful and arrogant in their positions of authority, making their positions about themselves. Matthew 23:11 (AMP) says, ***"But the greatest among you will be your servant. Whoever exalts himself***

CHAPTER 6 : THE POSITIONING OF HIS GIFTS

shall be humbled; and whoever humbles himself shall be raised to honor." God desires for his people to walk in a place of humility.

I learned this very valuable lesson in my early twenties as a new believer. You see, in my profession, I have always worked very hard and been good at what I do. As a result, I was often given positions of authority or promoted in a short amount of time. In many cases, I was the youngest person on staff or had to supervise people with much more experience. This sometimes caused a great deal of conflict, and I would run to God in prayer for wisdom. I would attempt to seek help from those who had put me in the positions, but I was often left to figure it out on my own. I particularly remember giving an instruction to an employee, thinking I was being fair and speaking kindly. The employee quickly barked at me, "Who do you think you are? I am not going to listen to you." I was embarrassed, of course, and ready to fight by using my authority to make this person do what I had said. I thought, "How dare she talk to me that way?" Unfortunately, I did not speak what I was thinking, but there was a heated discussion that was quite frankly fruitless. I left work that day asking what I could have done better. Was it me? This was not the first instance of what I thought was disrespect; however, it just seemed to all come down on me that week.

That week in prayer I brought my frustrations to the Lord. Through prayer and in my devotion time, God gave me two scriptures. The first was James 4:10 (AMP): *"Humble yourselves [with an attitude of repentance and insignificance] in the presence of the Lord, and He will exalt you [He will lift you up, He will give you purpose]."* The second was Jeremiah 31:3 (AMP): *"The Lord hath appeared of old unto me, saying, Yea, I have loved thee with an everlasting love: therefore with lovingkindness have I drawn thee."* When I pondered these two scriptures, I thought, "Lord, why am I wrong? They said this to me, she said that to me." But as I studied these scriptures, God revealed to me the pride that was in my heart. What I learned from these verses, which eventually came to guide me as a leader in my career, was the importance of walking in humility and love. You see, my way was to engage in power struggles to assert my authority, until the Lord showed me how to walk in humility and love.

I learned that walking in these two things was not about not having expectations or requiring compliance, but about beginning with relationship building and service to those I led. Through those experiences, God was teaching me true servant leadership. In God's direction I gained so much respect from those I served and experienced such a cohesiveness within my teams as I began to implement his instruction. God taught me the importance of being intentional about portraying his goodness and character in all my endeavors. When God positions his people in authority, we must understand that his divine plan is at work in and through us. The Bible says in Proverbs 29:11 (Message), **"When good people run things, everyone is glad, but when the ruler is bad, everyone groans."** As a result of this lesson I purchased a plaque with the scripture James 4:10 engraved on it. I placed it in my office and read that scripture each day I came to work. It was a constant reminder to walk in humility. God gives us all gifts and talents that can be manifested in our jobs, businesses, ministries and communities. We must be very careful to live a submitted life to God so that we can exemplify his goodness, essence and nature. He causes the influence and impact of his people to be expanded on earth for the advancement of his kingdom. Our divine portrayal of our heavenly father is fulfilled through true servanthood, which ultimately brings the kingdom of heaven down to earth.

CHAPTER 6 : THE POSITIONING OF HIS GIFTS

God's positioning enables the spirit-filled believer to experience growth and maturity, which leads to God-like character and the ability to transform lives. Transformation in the lives of his people is truly God's infinite imagination fulfilled through servanthood.

PRAYER:

Father, I pray for your people. I pray that you will continue to keep them in your perfect peace as their mind is stayed on you. Father, you equipped your people with strength for battle and you have caused all things that are against your people to sink. Thank you, God. Thank you that no weapon formed against your people shall prosper.

God, you are so good to your people. You know just what they need and when they need it. Your timing is perfect. Father, thank you that you are causing all things to work together for their good as they are called according to your purpose. Father, cause your people to hear your voice and be sensitive to your move in their lives. Cause them not to be deceived by the opinion of man and their own sense of timing, but give your people the capacity to wait on you. I declare that they will not grow weary in their well doing, for in due season they will reap if they faint not. Father, cause your people not to faint.

Father, I declare that your people will trust in you with all their hearts, and will not lean on their own understanding. I declare that in all their ways they will acknowledge you, and you will make straight their paths. Father, thank you for your guidance and provision. Father, you have made everything beautiful and appropriate in its time. You have planted eternity and a sense of divine purpose in the hearts of your people. Father, there is a longing which nothing under the sun can satisfy, except you. Glory to God. Cause your people to gain a greater understanding of the longing in their hearts and guide them to a clear path in purpose.

Father, remove the erroneous Christian doctrine that has crippled your people from embracing the fullness of you, to enable them to be positioned as you have ordained. Take the scales off of the eyes of your people and cause them to be transformed by the renewing of their minds in Christ Jesus.

Father, thank you that your people's time is in your hands. We thank you that you do not delay and are not slow to fulfill your promise for the lives of the people. Thank you. Father, I thank you that as your people move forward, you will supply all the needs of your people according to the riches in glory of Christ Jesus. Hallelujah!

In Jesus's name... Amen.

CHAPTER 7
The Promise That Lies in His Gifts

God's promises are longer than life, broader than sin, deeper than the grave and higher than the clouds.

~C. H. Spurgeon

God has given the spirit-filled believer a guarantee, promising peace, provision, protection and providence. Through his Word, God has promised us that not only will he save us but he will provide what we need for a good life. John 10:9-10 (AMP) says, *"I am the Door; anyone who enters through Me will be saved [and will live forever], and will go in and out [freely], and find pasture (spiritual security). The thief comes only in order to steal and kill and destroy. I came that they may have and enjoy life, and have it in abundance [to the full, till it overflows]."* God's desire for his children is fulfillment, joy and satisfaction in life. Experiencing true fulfillment and satisfaction can be one of the biggest challenges of man—often because we look for them in all the wrong spaces.

God's promises are guaranteed in the life of a spirit-filled believer, but how easily we can access them depends on how we choose to live. Although he desires for his people to have a willing heart and to obey him, God grants his servants free will. When we don't obey God's voice, we often find ourselves in difficult circumstances and out of season with his perfect will for our lives. God's voice and presence in our life are like a navigational system that enables direction throughout each of our journeys. Proverbs 3:5-6 says, *"Trust in and rely confidently on the Lord with all your heart. And do not rely on your own insight or understanding. In all your ways know and acknowledge and recognize Him, and He will make your paths straight and smooth [removing obstacles that block your way]."* Throughout this book, we have talked about the power that is in God's propelling, placement and positioning on earth, but we must not miss the very essential point that all these things are contingent upon our willingness to allow him to order our steps. Proverbs 20:24 says, *"Man's steps are ordered and ordained by the Lord. How then can a man [fully] understand his way?"* We understand God's way by increasing our communion with him and spending time in his Word, where we are provided wisdom, knowledge and his promises that give the spirit-filled believer confidence and courage to embark upon their God-ordained journey.

God promises peace to his children and desires us to see him as the source and sustainer of our lives. If he has sent us to earth to fulfill his plan, why would he not then provide all that we need as we proceed with that plan? Let's look at the promise of peace God has provided in his Word. Philippians 4:6–7 (AMP) says, **"Do not be anxious or worried about anything, but in everything [every circumstance and situation], by prayer and petition with thanksgiving, continue to make your [specific] requests known to God. And the peace of God [that peace which reassures the heart, that peace] which transcends all understanding, [that peace which] stands guard over your hearts and your minds in Christ Jesus [is yours]."** In this scripture, God has made it clear that he wants us not to worry and to come to him with our prayers. He wants us to acknowledge his goodness through praise so that he can sustain us. Our promises in God require our continued trust that God is able to sustain us in our purpose as his plan is manifested in our lives.

Experiencing peace is crucial for the believer; it is essential to our ability to maintain focus on our assignment and the journey that God has positioned us in. Maintaining that peace requires continually seeking God and his Word. It is through his Word that we are given the wisdom to pursue a more fulfilled life. In 2 Peter 1:3, the Bible assures us that **"his divine power hath given unto us all things that pertain unto life and godliness, through the knowledge of him that hath called us to glory and virtue"**—in this, we are given the assurance that in each of our lives there is a power source enabling us to accomplish all things. Glory to God, his promise has a lifetime guarantee.

God has given his spirit-filled believer the promise of provision. As we seek him in all things and follow his lead, he will provide for us. God is so invested in his gifts and the plan for our lives that he grants us sufficiency in all things as we are activated in our journey. Philippians 4:19 says, **"But my God shall supply all your needs according to his riches in glory by Christ Jesus."** This should provide confidence that if we are clear on God's purpose and assignment in our lives, we already have what we need. We don't need to obtain it, because he has already given it to us. However, we do have to be acquainted with who he is. Knowledge of God helps us to detect his direction and the grace that comes in our journey. If we are not acquainted with God's way and able to hear his voice, we are not able to experience God in the fullness that he desires. The challenge for the spirit-filled believer is to be able to see his provision and care, even when it looks different than what you expect or does not come in the way in which you would like it to. Because God knows all and he can see further than us, he has the advantage and is able to provide the perfect intervention needed for our success and growth. We, again, just need to trust him. To learn more about how to develop a more intimate relationship with the Lord and gain the capacity to recognize his voice, I suggest that you read my book *F.I.G.H.T.*

God promises protection to his people. This is not the kind of protection that guarantees nothing uncomfortable or bad will happen in our lives or that we won't face obstacles on our journeys of purpose, but an assurance that he will always be with us. God will allow us the strength and capacity to endure hardships knowing that he is there waiting to be a strength in our weakness. Let's look at Isaiah 43:2 (NIV): **"When you pass through the**

waters, I will be with you; and when you pass through the rivers, they will not sweep over you. When you walk through the fire, you will not be burned; the flames will not set you ablaze." This scripture lets us know that whatever obstacles we face on our journey, through it all, God will be with us. When I think about the promise of protection from our heavenly father, I think of a shield, a shelter, a screen, a defense, a buffer. Think about the times in your life God acted as a buffer to protect you from significant pain. This is the promise he makes to us—that he will act as a buffer in our lives to prevent destruction and our demise. Psalm 121:7–8 (NIV) says that ***"the Lord will keep you from all harm—he will watch over your life; the Lord will watch over your coming and going both now and forevermore."***

God promises providence for his people. When you look at the definition of *providence* in *Oxford Languages*, it is the spiritual power from God that preserves his people, and it is also "timely preparation for future eventualities." With these definitions, we understand that not only does God give us the spiritual power necessary to keep us, he also equips us supernaturally for what is to come. God's promises make him accountable and responsible to his people and to their ends. We are not always aware of how God will provide or of whom he will use to help us, but those are details better left to him, the all-sufficient one. God desires us to seek his face and believe that he will take care of us. We must trust God's promise that guarantees his faithfulness and provision for our lives. Hebrews 11:6 (NLT) says, ***"And it is impossible to please God without faith. Anyone who wants to come to him must believe that God exists and that he rewards those who sincerely seek him."*** The Word challenges us to believe God and take him at his word literally despite how things may look. In God's wisdom, power, righteousness and love, he is committed to carrying out the eternal purpose that he has established for our eternal good.

The promises of God are an assurance that each spirit-filled believer is equipped with the power of God and all the resources they need to fulfill the divine plan of the father. Through his Word, God has so richly given us a road map that enables us to gain insight into his heart and mind concerning all of earth. Our ability to obey God's word determines the experiences we have and whether or not we maintain the capacity to fulfill his assignment, but nothing can negate his promises of provision, protection and the endowment of his spiritual gifts. When we do not obey God, our way may be more difficult, but God's love and his promise to be with us always will never falter. Proverbs 13:15 (KJV) says, **"Good understanding giveth favour: but the way of transgressors is hard."** Just because our way may be more difficult than necessary, it does not mean that God's promise of provision won't keep us and help guide us through. While this is not a license to not obey God, it is crucial that we understand the faithfulness of our father and the power that lies in his promises for his gifts.

PRAYER:

Father, thank you for your promises. Thank you for your faithfulness and your Word that is your people's daily bread. Father, thank you for your covenant that has enabled your people to be seated in heavenly places in Christ Jesus. Thank you for your provision, protection and providence in our lives. You are a sustainer of life, you are a shield to your people and a comforter during the most difficult times. Father,

thank you for your promises that have made your people to be partakers of your divine nature. Thank you. Father, I pray that your people will develop a greater capacity to receive your promises and that your confessions will become a part of their daily confessions.

Father, I pray that your people will not be paralyzed by their former natures but they will willingly embrace the truth of your Word. I declare that your Word is fortifying them. Father, you are a sun and shield; you bestow favor and honor. Thank you that there is no good thing that you will withhold from those who walk uprightly in you. Thank you for the promise of your Word!

In Jesus's name... Amen.

Conclusion

God has sent his gifts, which are his people, to earth to exemplify his essence, nature and glory. In this book, we have been on a journey through the heart and mind of God as it relates to servanthood and his divine plan for his people on earth. It is only through the Word of God that his people are able to understand his mind and thoughts concerning creation. As God's representatives and carriers of his glory, we are equipped with all the spiritual blessings necessary to have the life that God has designed for us on earth. As his gifts, we are to operate and function as gods on earth with the power and authority to bring heaven down on earth and to reestablish his kingdom on earth.

As kingdom citizens, we possess the best of both worlds, the heavenly and the earthly. In Revelation 5:10 (KJV), it says, **"and hast made us unto our God kings and priests: and we shall reign on the earth."** God in his sovereignty has given us the ability to bring heaven to earth by exemplifying his nature and essence and fulfilling his ultimate plan. As kings and priests, we have the rights and privileges that come with royalty. We are true carriers of his glory with divine authority in our mouths and in our works. Through this authority, the infinite imagination of our heavenly father is fulfilled through our servanthood.

Thank you so much for taking the time to read this book. My prayer is that you have gained a greater understanding of God's infinite plan for your life and that you are on your way to discovering purpose. And if you have already discovered your God-given purpose, my desire is that you will gain the capacity to see yourself with greater depth and substance. That you will begin to see the power you possess and the impact God has designed for you to have on earth. You are his divine original. I pray that you are able to grasp just how much God loves you and how he carefully designed you to be a conduit of his grace and love to all mankind.

Scripture References

Psalm 24 (KJV) – *"The earth is the LORD's, and the fulness thereof; the world, and they that dwell therein."*

Matthew 20:28 (AMP) – *"Just as the Son of Man did not come to be served, but to serve, and to give His life as a ransom for many [paying the price to set them free from the penalty of sin]..."*

Chapter 1

Genesis 1:26–28 (AMP) – *"Then God said, "Let Us (Father, Son, Holy Spirit) make man in Our image, according to Our likeness [not physical, but a spiritual personality and moral likeness]; and let them have complete authority over the fish of the sea, the birds of the air, the cattle, and over the entire earth, and over everything that creeps and crawls on the earth." So God created man in His own image, in the image and likeness of God He created him; male and female He created them. And God blessed them [granting them certain authority] and said to them, "Be fruitful, multiply, and fill the earth, and subjugate it [putting it under your power]; and rule over (dominate) the fish of the sea, the birds of the air, and every living thing that moves upon the earth."*

1 Corinthians 15:49 – *"Just as we have borne the image of the earthly [the man of dust], we will also bear the image of the heavenly [the Man of heaven]."*

1 John 4:7 (AMP) – *"Beloved, let us [unselfishly] love and seek the best for one another, for love is from God; and everyone who loves [others] is born of God and knows God [through personal experience]."*

1 John 4:8 (AMP) - *"The one who does not love has not become acquainted with God [does not and never did know Him], for God is love. [He is the originator of love, and it is an enduring attribute of His nature.]"*

1 John 4:12 (AMP) – *"No one has seen God at any time. But if we love one another [with unselfish concern], God abides in us, and His love [the love that is His essence abides in us and] is completed and perfected in us."*

Romans 1:20 (AMP) – *"For ever since the creation of the world His invisible attributes, His eternal power and divine nature, have been clearly seen, being understood through His workmanship [all His creation, the wonderful things that He has made], so that they [who fail to believe and trust in Him] are without excuse and without defense."*

Isaiah 11:2 (AMP) – *"The life-giving Spirit of God will hover over him, the Spirit that brings wisdom and understanding, the Spirit that gives direction and builds strength, the Spirit that instills knowledge and fear of God."*

Psalm 115:16 (TPT) – *"The heaven of heavens is for God, but he put us in charge of the earth."*

Jeremiah 1:5 (AMP) – *"Before I formed you in the womb I knew you [and approved of you as My chosen instrument], and before you were born I consecrated you [to Myself as My own]; I have appointed you as a prophet to the nations."*

Colossians 3:23-24 (AMP) – *"Whatever you do, work at it with all your heart, as working for the Lord, not for human masters, since you know that you will receive an inheritance from the Lord as a reward. It is the Lord Christ you are serving."*

Psalm 8:6 (NLT) – *"You gave them charge of everything you made, putting all things under their authority."*

Chapter 2

Jeremiah 1:5 (AMP) – *"Before I formed you in the womb I knew you [and approved of you as My chosen instrument], and before you were born I consecrated you [to Myself as My own]; I have appointed you as a prophet to the nations."*

Psalm 139:13-17 (AMP) – *"For You formed my innermost parts; You knit me [together] in my mother's womb. I will give thanks and praise to You, for I am fearfully and wonderfully made; wonderful are Your works, and my soul knows it very well. My frame was not hidden from You, when I was being formed in secret, and intricately and skillfully formed [as if embroidered with many colors] in the depths of the earth. Your eyes have seen my unformed substance; and in Your book were all written. The days were appointed for me, when as yet there was not one of them [even taking shape]. How precious also are Your thoughts to me, O God! How vast is the sum of them!"*

Colossians 1:16 (AMP) – *"For by Him all things were created in heaven and on earth, [things] visible and invisible, whether thrones or dominions or rulers or authorities; all things were created and exist through Him [that is, by His activity] and for Him."*

Lamentations 3:37–39 (AMP) – *"Who is there who speaks and it comes to pass, unless the Lord has authorized and commanded it? Is it not from the mouth of the Most High that both adversity (misfortune) and good (prosperity, happiness) proceed?"*

Matthew 28:18–20 (AMP) – *"All authority (all power of absolute rule) in heaven and on earth has been given to Me. Go therefore and make disciples of all the nations [help the people to learn of Me, believe in Me, and obey My words], baptizing them in the name of the Father and of the Son and of the Holy Spirit, teaching them to observe everything that I have commanded you; and lo, I am with you always [remaining with you perpetually—regardless of circumstance, and on every occasion], even to the end of the age."*

Luke 10:19–20 – *"Listen carefully: I have given you authority [that you now possess] to tread on serpents and scorpions, and [the ability to exercise authority] over all the power of the enemy (Satan); and nothing will [in any way] harm you. Nevertheless do not rejoice at this, that the spirits are subject to you, but rejoice that your names are recorded in heaven."*

Romans 8:19 (AMP) – *"For [even the whole] creation [all nature] waits eagerly for the children of God to be revealed."*

CHAPTER 3

1 Corinthians 12:7 (AMP) – *"But to each one is given the manifestation of the Spirit [the spiritual illumination and the enabling of the Holy Spirit] for the common good."*

1 Timothy 1:7 (Message) – *"God doesn't want us to be shy with his gifts, but bold and loving and sensible."*

Ephesians 2:10 (NIV) – *"For we are God's handiwork, created in Christ Jesus to do good works, which God prepared in advance for us to do."*

2 Corinthians 4:7 (NIV) – *"But we have this treasure in jars of clay to show that this all-surpassing power is from God and not from us."*

Acts 2:18 (NLT) – *In those days I will pour out my Spirit even on my servants—men and women alike—and they will prophesy."*

Psalm 115:16 (NIV) – *"The highest heavens belong to the Lord, but the earth he has given to mankind."*

1 Corinthians 12:4–12 (AMP) – *"Now there are [distinctive] varieties of spiritual gifts [special abilities given by the grace and extraordinary power of the Holy Spirit operating in believers], but it is the same Spirit [who grants them and empowers believers]. And there are [distinctive] varieties of ministries and service, but it is the same Lord [who is served]. And there are [distinctive] ways of working [to accomplish things], but it is the same God who produces all things in all believers [inspiring, energizing, and empowering them]. But to each one is given the manifestation of the Spirit [the spiritual illumination and the enabling of the Holy Spirit] for the common good. To one is given through the [Holy] Spirit [the power to speak] the message of wisdom, and to another [the power to express] the word of knowledge and understanding according to the same Spirit; to another [wonder-working] faith [is given] by the same [Holy] Spirit, and to another the [extraordinary] gifts of healings by the one Spirit; and to another the working of miracles, and to another prophecy [foretelling the future, speaking a new message from God to the people], and to another discernment of spirits [the ability to distinguish sound, godly doctrine from the deceptive doctrine of man-made religions*

and cults], to another various kinds of [unknown] tongues, and to another interpretation of tongues. All these things [the gifts, the achievements, the abilities, the empowering] are brought about by one and the same [Holy] Spirit, distributing to each one individually just as He chooses."

Romans 12:6–8 (AMP) – *"Since we have gifts that differ according to the grace given to us, each of us is to use them accordingly: if [someone has the gift of] prophecy, [let him speak a new message from God to His people] in proportion to the faith possessed; if service, in the act of serving; or he who teaches, in the act of teaching; or he who encourages, in the act of encouragement; he who gives, with generosity; he who leads, with diligence; he who shows mercy [in caring for others], with cheerfulness."*

Psalm 24:1 (AMP) – *"The earth is the Lord's, and the fullness of it, The world, and those who dwell in it."*

Ephesians 3:20 (AMP) – *"Now to Him who is able to [carry out His purpose and] do superabundantly more than all that we dare ask or think [infinitely beyond our greatest prayers, hopes or dreams], according to His power that is at work within us."*

CHAPTER 4

Romans 12:6 (AMP) – *"Since we have gifts that differ according to the grace given to us, each of us is to use them accordingly."*

Genesis 8:22 (AMP) – *"While the earth remains, seedtime and harvest, cold and heat, winter and summer, and day and night shall not cease."*

Psalm 74:17 (ESV) – *"You have fixed all the boundaries of the earth; you have made summer and winter."*

Psalm 8:6 (NLT) – *"You gave them charge of everything you made, putting all things under their authority."*

Ephesians 4:9-13 (AMP) – *"Now this expression, 'He ascended,' what does it mean except that He also had previously descended [from the heights of heaven] into the lower parts of the earth? He who descended is the very same as He who also has ascended high above all the heavens, that He [His presence] might fill all things [that is, the whole universe]). And [His gifts to the church were varied and] He Himself appointed some as apostles [special messengers, representatives], some as prophets [who speak a new message from God to the people], some as evangelists [who spread the good news of salvation], and some as pastors and teachers [to shepherd and guide and instruct], [and He did this] to fully equip and perfect the saints (God's people) for works of service, to build up the body of Christ [the church]; until we all reach oneness in the faith and in the knowledge of the Son of God, [growing spiritually] to become a mature believer, reaching to the measure of the fullness of Christ [manifesting His spiritual completeness and exercising our spiritual gifts in unity]."*

CHAPTER 5

Romans 5:3-4 (AMP) – *"And not only this, but [with joy] let us exult in our sufferings and rejoice in our hardships, knowing that hardship (distress, pressure, trouble) produces patient endurance; and endurance, proven character (spiritual maturity); and proven character, hope and confident assurance [of eternal salvation]."*

Romans 8:28 (AMP) – *"And we know [with great confidence] that God [who is deeply concerned about us] causes all things to work together [as a plan] for good for those who love God, to those who are called according to His plan and purpose."*

1 Peter 1:23 (AMP) – *"For you have been born again [that is, reborn from above—spiritually transformed, renewed, and set apart for His purpose] not of seed which is perishable but [from that which is] imperishable and immortal, that is, through the living and everlasting word of God."*

Proverbs 27:17 (AMP) – *"As iron sharpens iron, so one man sharpens [and influences] another [through discussion]."*

1 Peter 4:10 – *"Just as each one of you has received a special gift [a spiritual talent, an ability graciously given by God], employ it in serving one another as [is appropriate for] good stewards of God's multi-faceted grace [faithfully using the diverse, varied gifts and abilities granted to Christians by God's unmerited favor]."*

CHAPTER 6

Romans 8:28 (NLT) – *"And we know that God causes everything to work together for the good of those who love God and are called according to his purpose for them."*

Proverbs 3:5–6 (AMP) – *"Trust in and rely confidently on the Lord with all your heart and do not rely on your own insight or understanding. In all your ways know and acknowledge and recognize Him, and He will make your paths straight and smooth [removing obstacles that block your way]."*

Jeremiah 29:11 (AMP) – *"'For I know the plans and thoughts that I have for you,' says the Lord, 'plans for peace and well-being and not for disaster, to give you a future and a hope.'"*

Psalm 37:23 (AMP) – *"The steps of a [good and righteous] man are directed and established by the Lord, And He delights in his way [and blesses his path]."*

Psalm 139:8 (KJV) – *"If I ascend up into heaven, thou art there: if I make my bed in hell, behold, thou art there."*

Genesis 12:2-3 (NIV) – *"I will make you into a great nation, and I will bless you; I will make your name great, and you will be a blessing. I will bless those who bless you, and whoever curses you I will curse; and all peoples on earth will be blessed through you."*

Psalm 34:19 (AMP) – *"Many hardships and perplexing circumstances confront the righteous, but the Lord rescues him from them all."*

Psalm 75:6-7 (KJV) – *"For promotion cometh neither from the east, nor from the west, nor from the south. But God is the judge: he putteth down one, and setteth up another."*

Proverbs 21:5 (AMP) – *"The plans of the diligent lead surely to abundance and advantage, but everyone who acts in haste comes surely to poverty."*

Colossians 3:23 – *"Whatever you do [whatever your task may be], work from the soul [that is, put in your very best effort], as [something done] for the Lord and not for men."*

Proverbs 2:20-21 (AMP) – *"So you will walk in the way of good men [that is, those of personal integrity, moral courage and honorable character], and keep to the paths of the righteous. For the upright [those who are in right standing with God] will live in the land and those [of integrity] who are blameless [in God's sight] will remain in it."*

Matthew 23:11 (AMP) – *"But the greatest among you will be your servant. Whoever exalts himself shall be humbled; and whoever humbles himself shall be raised to honor."*

James 4:10 (AMP) – *"Humble yourselves [with an attitude of repentance and insignificance] in the presence of the Lord, and He will exalt you [He will lift you up, He will give you purpose]."*

Jeremiah 31:3 (AMP) – *"The Lord hath appeared of old unto me, saying, Yea, I have loved thee with an everlasting love: therefore with lovingkindness have I drawn thee."*

Proverbs 29:11 (Message) – *"When good people run things, everyone is glad, but when the ruler is bad, everyone groans."*

Chapter 7

John 10:9–10 (AMP) – *"I am the Door; anyone who enters through Me will be saved [and will live forever], and will go in and out [freely], and find pasture (spiritual security). The thief comes only in order to steal and kill and destroy. I came that they may have and enjoy life, and have it in abundance [to the full, till it overflows]."*

Proverbs 3:5–6 – *"Trust in and rely confidently on the Lord with all your heart. And do not rely on your own insight or understanding. In all your ways know and acknowledge and recognize Him, and He will make your paths straight and smooth [removing obstacles that block your way]."*

Proverbs 20:24 – *"Man's steps are ordered and ordained by the Lord. How then can a man [fully] understand his way?"*

Philippians 4:6–7 (AMP) – *"Do not be anxious or worried about anything, but in everything [every circumstance and situation]* by prayer and petition with thanksgiving, continue to make your [specific] requests known to God. And the peace of God [that peace which reassures the heart, that peace] which transcends all understanding, [that peace which] stands guard over your hearts and your minds in Christ Jesus [is yours]."

2 Peter 1:3 – *"His divine power hath given unto us all things that pertain unto life and godliness, through the knowledge of him that hath called us to glory and virtue."*

Philippians 4:19 – *"But my God shall supply all your needs according to his riches in glory by Christ Jesus."*

Isaiah 43:2 (NIV) – *"When you pass through the waters, I will be with you; and when you pass through the rivers, they will not sweep over you. When you walk through the fire, you will not be burned; the flames will not set you ablaze."*

Psalm 121:7–8 (NIV) – *"The Lord will keep you from all harm—he will watch over your life; the Lord will watch over your coming and going both now and forevermore."*

Hebrews 11:6 (NLT) – *"And it is impossible to please God without faith. Anyone who wants to come to him must believe that God exists and that he rewards those who sincerely seek him."*

Proverbs 13:15 (KJV) – *"Good understanding giveth favour: but the way of transgressors is hard."*

Conclusion

Revelation 5:10 (KJV) – *"And hast made us unto our God kings and priests: and we shall reign on the earth."*

SOURCES

Enlow, Johnny. *The Seven Mountain Mantle: Receiving the Joseph Anointing to Reform Nations.* Creation House, 2009.

Merriam Webster Dictionary

Oxford Languages

About the Author

Ebony is a licensed therapist, author, speaker/trainer, entrepreneur and minister of the Gospel. She is gifted as a preacher/teacher and intercessor in the Body of Christ. Ebony is founder of Triple G Living: God Goals & Grind, an empowerment organization designed to educate, equip and empower people to live "Life on Purpose." Triple G Living is designed to help kingdom believers experience freedom from all forms of bondage and to discover their God-given purpose on earth. Ebony possesses a deep conviction based on Psalm 115:16, which declares: ***"The heaven, even the heavens, are the Lord's: but the earth hath he given to the children of men."*** This Word is the foundation of Triple G Living and rooted in the belief that whether in ministry, the marketplace, business or the community, God seeks to manifest his GLORY through the lives of his people. We are all ordained to be his **public servants!**

Ebony provides individual and group coaching and mental health counseling. She also provides training in the areas of mental health and personal and spiritual development. To reach Ebony for more resources or to purchase her first book, *F.I.G.H.T.: Flourishing In God's Hands & Timing—A Journey to Fulfillment In God*, go to:

TRIPLEGLIVING.COM

www.ingramcontent.com/pod-product-compliance
Lightning Source LLC
Chambersburg PA
CBHW070933080526
44589CB00013B/1501